In the Footsteps of
Anne Lister

In the Footsteps of Anne Lister

Travels of a remarkable English gentlewoman in
France, Germany and Denmark in 1833

Volume 1

Adeline Lim

First published 2021

Copyright © Adeline Lim, 2021

The moral right of the author has been asserted.

All rights reserved.

No part of this book may be reproduced, stored in a retrieval system, or transmitted, in any form or by any means, without the prior permission in writing of the author, nor be otherwise circulated in any form of binding or cover other than that in which it is published and without a similar condition including this condition being imposed on the subsequent purchaser.

Edited by Paul Roberts
Cover design by Sadie Butterworth-Jones
Maps and illustrations by Vincentas Saladis
Typeset by Leah Jespersen

Paperback ISBN: 9798702736280

For Ziggy Monster
(2004 – 2019)

If there is a heaven, it is certain our animals are to be there. Their lives become so interwoven with our own, it would take more than an archangel to detangle them.

Pam Brown

*Going abroad always likely to do good.
People should not grow mouldy at home.*

Anne Lister, 3 November 1834

Contents

Reading Anne Lister	xiii
Preface	xvii
Introduction	xxiii
Chapter One: Serendipity	1
Chapter Two: Shibden to Paris	9
Chapter Three: Paris to Luxembourg	35
Chapter Four: Trier to Einbeck	69
Chapter Five: Einbeck to Bremen	107
Chapter Six: Bremen to Copenhagen	131
Chapter Seven: Denmark	157
Chapter Eight: The Rush Home	201
Afterword	233
Acknowledgements	235
Anne Lister's Itinerary	239
About the Author	249

Maps

Anne Lister's journey in 1833   7

Anne Lister's route from
 Calais to Luxembourg in 1833   33

Anne Lister's route through
 Germany to Travemünde in 1833   67

Anne Lister's route home from
 Copenhagen in 1833   199

Reading Anne Lister

Anne Lister's nineteenth-century prose and terminology can sometimes be confounding to the modern reader. She wrote not only in old-fashioned English, but had her own version of *Franglais*, where she mixed French and English in one sentence. In addition, she abbreviated almost every word, which can regularly be interpreted in a variety of ways. The abbreviation of *natl* could be used for natural or national and *brd* for bread or broad. Her writing, though often neat, naturally varied according to her moods, becoming more illegible when she rushed or was upset.

Sometimes, she also wrote in her crypt hand, a series of symbols, numbers and alphabets with neither punctuation nor spacing between each word. While at first difficult to decode, when mastered, it was often a relief to transcribe rather than her plain hand.

In keeping her words as true to her writing as possible, I have made very few edits to the excerpts I have used, but where necessary have corrected spelling of names and added punctuation to aid the modern reader. Where *Franglais,* French, German or Latin came into play, I have provided a translation in the footnotes.

I have left the obsolete spellings she used as they were. For example, shew for show, staid for stayed, clipt for clipped, and tho' and thro' for though and through respectively. Where I have had to insert a word that Anne had accidentally left out, I have marked it with [...].

English currency during Anne's time was written in a particular format, e.g. 15/. for fifteen shillings, 15*s*/2*d* for fifteen shillings and two pennies and 1.15.2 or £1.15.2 to denote one pound, fifteen shillings and two pennies. I have left her quotes as they were but have used a simple form to convey currency, e.g. £15 and seventeen shillings in my text.

Anne used to tell time by writing in a format such as 11 20/60, for both 11.20 A.M. and P.M. But sometime in the third quarter of 1829 she started to drop the /60 for /.. very likely for efficiency. I have left her format unchanged in the quotes.

Some of the people Anne met had their names recorded in various spellings. For example, Sophie O'Ferral was spelt Ferrall and Ferral interchangeably. I have adopted

Ferral based on her sister, Countess Blücher's marriage and genealogy records, and records pertaining to her brother's ascension to the Danish Nobility as Count Ferral-Bourke. Peter Browne's name was at various occasions Browne or Brown, and Thorvaldsen recorded as Thorswalden. For the purpose of consistency, I have used the correct spelling in my text.

I have provided the West Yorkshire Archive Service's reference numbers for the extracts included in the book. Reference numbers prior to the 1833 trip are included as footnotes. From June to December 1833, the excerpts span from SH:7/ML/E/16/0068 to SH:7/ML/E/16/0151. All transcriptions in this book are my own, and I apologise for any errors I may have inadvertently made.

Preface

It was by fate's hand when I woke up one day and decided to click on BBC Online to read the news. I was living in Bonn, Germany, and I mainly read the news in German to improve my proficiency. But that spring morning, for some reason, I decided to visit BBC Online.

I sat, bleary-eyed and cradling a coffee at my desk when an article about a new BBC series called *Gentleman Jack* caught my attention. I clicked on the link. It told a story of a lady landowner in the 1800s, Anne Lister, who was determined to find herself a wife.

The storyline of the series followed Anne's return home to Shibden Hall in Halifax after a failed courtship of Vere Hobart in Hastings. She set her attention to improving her estate, developed plans for a coal mine on her lands and dealt with errant tenants in a no-nonsense manner, atypical of women of that period. Soon her attention was diverted by a sweet but tentative neighbour, Ann Walker, who lived in Crow Nest about two and a half miles from her property.

I wasn't one to watch a lot of television. I had never heard of Anne Lister or the show's producer, Sally Wainwright, or Shibden Hall, Anne's home. There was a feature piece about Anne Lister published by the BBC, attached to the article about *Gentleman Jack*. I realised then that she was a very captivating character – a woman ahead of her time, strong, progressive, unashamedly lesbian, an adventuress and a remarkably prolific diarist. In 2011, her diaries were added to the UNESCO *Memory of the World* register, which described her as '*a remarkable landowner, business woman, intrepid traveller, mountaineer and lesbian*'[1].

Through this, I discovered she travelled – both extensively and intensively. It was this facet of her life that fascinated me most. Travelling on foot or on mules, by horse and carriage, steamboat, encumbered by heavy portmanteaus, layers of petticoats, Anne scaled mountains and visited feats of engineering, magical castles and awe-inspiring cities. During her travels she met famous and very interesting personalities, people who have since been immortalised in the annals of

---

1. https://www.unesco.org.uk/portfolio/memory-of-the-world/

history. These included Johann Friedrich Blumenbach, an elderly German physician best known for his work and study of comparative anatomy and scientific anti-racism, who she met in Göttingen in 1833 and described how he *'stoops a good deal, has a little rheumatism and is evidently un vieillard'*. There was August Wilhelm Schlegel, a linguistics professor celebrated for his translation of the Bhagavad Gita who she met in Bonn in 1829 and about whom she noted in her diary, *'really spoke very good English'*. In Geneva in 1827 she met Léonard Gaudin, *'a very intelligent, elderly man'*, renowned for his models and drawings of Switzerland's topography, and while in Copenhagen in 1833, she rubbed shoulders with the Danish royalty.

I was enthralled and thought to myself that I really should watch this *Gentleman Jack*. What was then an insignificant click of the mouse, I see now as serendipitous.

I had been house-bound since returning from London during the Christmas holidays of 2018. My dog, Ziggy, who was turning fifteen in July 2019 had been unwell for some time. At our hotel in London, I had to carry him down several flights of stairs to get from our room to the gardens. It was not an easy task as he weighed twenty kilogrammes, nearly half my own weight. I had then realised that Christmas was his last holiday. This made his walk along the beaches of Dunkerque, where we stopped prior to taking the Channel Tunnel from Calais, even more poignant.

Most of the latter part of 2018 into June 2019 was a blur of veterinarian appointments for him – his orthopaedic surgeon in Erftstadt, his cardiologist in Pulheim, his oncologist in Frankfurt and innumerable trips to his regular vet in Bonn. He was diagnosed with all the worst things I could imagine – melanoma, spondylosis, idiopathic chylothorax and severe arthritis. Yet, perhaps as a result of his cocktail of drugs, he lived a happy and full life. He was alert in mind and his appetite was as voracious as ever. I had known, when I left Sydney with him in January 2017, that his journey would be a one-way flight. I had planned to live in Germany for at least three years and knew there was no chance he would be alive when I made the return trip.

He had sauntered out of the Lufthansa lounge in Frankfurt, as though flying more than thirty hours was the most natural thing in the world. He adapted to life in Germany far quicker than I. In Australia, dogs are rarely allowed in hotels, never in restaurants or bars, or national parks, so I was very impressed when he seemed to take liberal Germany in his stride. While I had to juggle learning a new language, obtaining residency papers, setting up my home office and meeting new friends, he confidently pattered into a *bierhaus* or restaurant and charmed all the staff and then sat quietly or napped

Preface

under the table as I dined. He walked the halls of hotels as though he owned them. He even found a girlfriend for sleepovers, a bonny Labrador called Hummel.

Ziggy learned to ride on trams and elevators and conquered his fear of escalators. We would make a sprint towards the strange moving steps; then with a mighty leap, he would land on the escalators and gallop to the other end. He always received a big hug and applause every time he used the escalator. People must have thought me mad.

Together, we explored Europe. We strolled along the banks of the Rhine river, clambered over castle ruins in Germany, contemplated the Berlin wall, visited citadels in Belgium and explored the wine region of Alsace in France. When not travelling, he supervised me as I gardened at home, counter-surfed as I cooked and snored soporifically as I watched television or read.

When Ziggy passed in late June 2019, the television series was coming to an end. By then I had devoured the books about Anne Lister by Anne Choma, Helena Whitbread, Angela Steidele and Jill Liddington. In danger of spiralling into a darkness of grief, I rallied myself with a plan. I would follow in the footsteps of Anne Lister when she left Shibden in 1833 after suffering disappointment and heartbreak as a result of her failed courtship of Ann Walker, the heiress of Crow Nest. My journey, mapped with the help of Choma and

Steidele's biographies of Anne, was estimated to cover approximately two thousand kilometres over fourteen days.

Tracing her steps from south-western Germany, near the border of Luxembourg, my travels would take me through Trier, Koblenz, Marburg, Kassel and the university town of Göttingen. From there, I would head north to Hanover and Bremen, then north-east to Hamburg, Lübeck and Travemünde before crossing the Fehmarn Belt into Denmark. There, I planned to visit the sights she saw in Copenhagen and emulate her journey home through the Danish islands of Sjælland and Fyn and the Jutland peninsula back into Germany before arriving in Cuxhaven where her steamer, the Columbine, was moored for five days as a result of storms and repairs.

I realised then that an itinerary forcing me to get up every day intent on doing a certain prescribed number of things would give me a purpose and more importantly, a much-required distraction. Several days after his death, Ziggy's cremated remains were returned to me in a cream-coloured urn, which I placed on a shelf in my study. The very next day, Saturday, 6 July 2019, I packed my bags and got into the car.

It was to be a decision I would never regret.

Introduction

Anne Lister

Anne Lister was born to Jeremy and Rebecca Lister on Sunday, 3 April 1791, in Halifax in West Yorkshire, England. Between 1789 and 1798, the Listers had six children, four boys and two girls. Recent research has revealed that in 1806, a seventh child was born. It died in infancy; its gender undisclosed. Anne's brothers all died young. The eldest, John, was only seven weeks old when he passed away in 1789, and the longest-living male sibling, Samuel, drowned when he was overcome by the current of the Blackwater, near Fermoy in Cork County, Ireland[1]. He was twenty years old. By the middle of 1813, of the seven Lister offspring, only Anne and her younger sister, Marian, were left.

---

1. British Newspaper Archive – Nottingham Gazette, 16 July 1813

Anne was educated through a combination of private tutors at home, schooling in Agnesgate, Ripon, and at Manor House in York, which she attended for a year in 1805. She possessed a brilliant mind, but did not always apply herself in her studies, and by her own admission, *'was always a great pickle. Never learnt anything at school. Was always talking to the girls instead of attending to my book*[2]*'*. When Anne was expelled from the Manor House in 1806 – very likely for unbecoming conduct with Eliza Raine, her first lesbian lover – she became more estranged with her mother, who was an alcoholic. However, she found comfort and affection with her Aunt Anne and Uncle James at Shibden Hall, an estate forty miles west of York. Her formal schooling recommenced at home in 1808, tutored by Reverend Samuel Knight. A precocious and intelligent girl, she devoured everything. Her curriculum ranged from Greek to mathematics, French to philosophy. Anything that could be taught was absorbed.

She never stopped learning – even as an adult, traipsing through the European continent. She would be armed with her trusty handbooks, published by the leading authorities of the period, such as Galignani, Johann Gottfried Ebel and John Murray. She visited schools and hospitals and recorded her observations in her travel journals and diaries. Her notes on the

---

2. 10 March 1819 – WYAS SH:7/ML/E/2/0117

renowned Hofwil school, founded by Philipp Emanuel von Fellenberg in the outskirts of Bern in Switzerland, ran into three pages – about two thousand words. Later in 1833, while in Denmark, she tried to master German. Much to her despair her progress was slow, not aided by the fact that she kept falling asleep over her studies.

She critically appraised the architecture of buildings and compared churches to the York Minster. They often fell short. She assessed Milan cathedral as *'very fine, but York Cathedral spoils me*[3]*'*. Of the resplendent Reims Cathedral, even though she was *'never more pleased with a church'* and that it was *'worth coming to Reims to see this cathedral'*, the building was unfortunately *'not so fine as York Minster*[4]*'*. She visited cheese manufacturers in Switzerland. She went down all sorts of mines, including those that produced salt, coal and silver. She was also an enthusiastic mountaineer. In 1830, she scaled Mont Perdu and in August 1838 she became the first person to summit Vignemale. At 3,298 metres, nearly 11,000 feet, it is the highest summit in the French Pyrenees. In 1827, while on tour in the Swiss Alps with her lover, Maria Barlow, she traversed the passes of the Furka, Grimsel, Splügen, Simplon, Gotthard and the Great Saint Bernard sometimes knee-deep in snow, side-stepping crevasses. During that same tour, she travelled from Geneva to

---

3. 9 August 1827 – WYAS SH:7/ML/TR/1/0068
4. 25 May 1838 – WYAS SH:7/ML/E/21/0108

Chamonix to visit the Chamonix Valley's *Mer de Glace*, the largest glacier in France.

Her experiences and thoughts were recorded faithfully in her travel journals. So too were distances travelled and the time taken, temperature, the cost of the horses and coachmen, accommodation, the honesty of innkeepers, what she ate, at what time, how much it cost and if she enjoyed it or not. '*I shall always be sure as I travel along that my observations, when made at the instant, are correct, at least as far as they can be so*[5]'. Anne also had a bizarrely macabre enthusiasm for recording how people of the places she visited had died, including the causes of death which ranged from accidents to murders or lawful sentencing. Her obsessive nature now provides us with an accurate and in-depth account of what conditions of travel were like in the 1800s.

Over a span of time exceeding two decades, Anne wrote more than twenty volumes – thick, quality-bound tomes filled with her neat, but near-illegible scrawl. Intriguingly, she also used a secret crypt hand she once thought was indecipherable. Her diaries, travel journals, notes and letters languished for decades, hidden behind panels in her home. They were found by John Lister, a relative whose father had inherited Shibden Hall. He published more than a hundred articles about Halifax, based on what he could understand from the plain hand

---

5. 2 September 1822 – WYAS SH:7/ML/E/6/0048

in her diaries. In the late nineteenth century, John Lister and his friend, Arthur Burrell, managed to decode her crypt hand. The revelation of Anne's most private and inner thoughts proved too abhorrent and scandalous to publish. Homosexuality was only decriminalised in England in 1967, and although sex between women was never subject to the same law, it was still considered deplorable. John Lister stopped publishing Anne's diaries and put them back behind the panels of Shibden Hall where he had first found them. There they waited once again. Only providence would decree when they would see the light of day again.

In 1923, John Lister was declared bankrupt. A Halifax councillor, Arthur McCrea, bought the property and presented its ninety acres of parkland to the townspeople of east Halifax. It was opened as a public park by the Prince of Wales in 1926. John Lister was able to live out his life undisturbed at the Hall, and upon his death in 1933, the property was bequeathed to the Halifax Corporation which opened it as a museum in 1934[6]. Anne's journals were retrieved and archived. They now reside at the West Yorkshire Archive Service in Halifax, less than a mile's walk from Anne's old home.

---

6. Source: Historic England

Anne Lister is famous for being the *'first modern lesbian'*. Her diaries include sections written in crypt hand of her relationships and sexual conquests – an astonishingly candid account of her sex life and sometimes, even a rating of whether the sex was *'good, goodish, very good'* or *'tolerable'*. She had her own euphemisms to describe certain sexual and anatomical concepts. An orgasm was termed *'a kiss'*, *'queer'* was used for the vagina or vulva, pubic hair was *'moustaches'*, masturbation was *'incurring a cross'* and sex by digital stimulation or penetration was *'grubbling'*.

Her first sexual relationship was with Eliza Raine, an attractive girl from Anne's time in boarding school at Manor House, York. They were both allocated the attic bedroom in the school likely because neither conformed to societal norms of the time. Anne was a precocious tomboy and Eliza, whose mother was Indian, was considered foreign and perhaps too exotic. It was with Eliza that Anne established her crypt hand in 1806. It was a collection of symbols, alphabets and numbers designed in order to correspond privately with Eliza and to record her own intimate and private thoughts in her diary.

As with all young first loves, her ardour for Eliza diminished as time and other distractions created a widening chasm between them. In 1810, Anne met Isabella Norcliffe while living in York. They became fast friends and soon, lovers. In 1812, Anne met Mariana

Belcombe, who became an enduring passion for her. With Anne entranced by Mariana, she grew even more distant from Eliza. However, her union with Mariana did not have a happy ending, with Mariana marrying Charles Lawton in March 1816. Mariana's marriage to Charles, nineteen years her senior, was for convenience, not love. She came from a family of modest means and her father, a doctor, had sired six children. Five of them were girls and had to be married off to respectable men of means. If Mariana had not married, she would have been penniless. Anne, in 1816, had yet to inherit Shibden and was uncertain of her financial status. It was not uncommon to hear of spinsters living together in the nineteenth century, consolidating their living expenses, but Anne was just twenty-five and Mariana nearly twenty-six. They were hardly what one could categorise as old spinsters. Though devastated by the thought of losing Mariana, Anne realised that she could not ask her to turn down Charles's proposal. Charles was instrumental in providing Mariana's future with financial security. Perhaps Anne thought that, should Charles die, she and Mariana could live out their lives together with what Mariana inherited.

In any case, the heartbreak resulting from Mariana and Charles's marriage did not stop Anne from continuing her sexual relationship with Mariana or pursuing new lovers. By the latter part of 1816, Anne was successfully wooing Mariana's elder sister, Anne Belcombe, whom they endearingly referred to as Nantz. The affair fizzled out, however, they kept in each other's orbit within York society. In 1818, Anne commenced an intimate relationship with Mary Vallance, with whom she had been acquainted since 1817 through Isabella's mother, Ann Norcliffe. In 1821, Anne contracted what she assumed was venereal disease from Mariana. Charles Lawton's past or continuing dalliances were blamed and Anne surreptitiously sought treatment from Mariana's brother, Steph Belcombe, who, like his father, was a physician.

In the years following the Napoleonic Wars, travel between England and the Continent opened up again. In 1819, Anne and her aunt travelled to Paris, their first foray to the European continent. She travelled to France again in early September 1822 with her father, Jeremy, and sister, Marian. Jeremy Lister was considering moving to France as a cheaper alternative to living in England. The trip however, seemed like Anne's worst nightmare. Jeremy and Marian lacked her stamina for walking and enthusiasm for foreign interests. Marian even took issue to how the French grew their potatoes. In the company of such sourpusses, Anne confided in her diary that being with them was *'dull work'* and that she *'felt solitary and forlorn. Marian, poor girl, is no society for me and I am thoroughly ashamed of my father's vulgarity'*. Anne was also despondent that her French was not good enough,

'I could hardly make myself understood at the library today and felt forlorn altogether'[7]. Finally, they all trudged home unhappily towards the end of September.

In 1824, in a bid to improve her French and seeking a cure from the complaint she had contracted from Mariana in 1821, Anne convinced her aunt and uncle to let her travel to Paris and live there. Anne was accompanied by her maid, Elizabeth Cordingley, who therefore provided an image of decorum for a respectable young lady travelling on her own. Arriving in Paris on 1 September, she stayed at Madame de Boyve's property in 24 Place Vendôme. There, Anne met Maria Barlow, a widow who was living in Paris with her young daughter, Jane, aged thirteen. Living costs were lower in France and Mrs Barlow was able to eke out her late husband's pension[8] well enough in Paris. By November of 1824, Anne and Mrs Barlow had started an intimate relationship, *'I had kissed and pressed Mrs Barlow on my knee till I had had a complete fit of passion'*[9]. But for all of Anne's wooing and seduction of Mrs Barlow, Anne knew deep down that her affair with a widow of no rank in society would come to nought. In January 1825, Anne and Mrs Barlow moved into 15 Quai Voltaire together – the first time Anne lived with another woman. Their union

---

7. 9 September 1822 – WYAS SH:7/ML/E/6/0052
8. Maria Barlow's husband's pension was £80 per year, with an additional supplement from the government of £250 – SH:7/ML/E/8/0046 (page 81)
9. 11 November 1824 – WYAS SH:7/ML/E/8/0076

was not without troubles. Mrs Barlow was perceptive of Anne's roving eye and did not appreciate the attention Anne was paying to a certain Mademoiselle de Sans. Anne had also confided in a dismayed Mrs Barlow about her relationships with Eliza Raine and Mariana Lawton, recording in her crypt hand that, *'Mrs Barlow, I expect, will not like to find herself not first with me[10]'*.

Despite Anne's misgivings about Mrs Barlow's place in society and possessiveness, it did not stop Anne from conducting a rather steamy relationship with her. In late March, just a few days prior to her departure from Paris, *'at about eleven and three quarters'*, Anne *'took her on my knee and began grubbling[11]. She having no support for her back, lay her on the bed. Knelt down by her, grubbled well and had the kiss[12]. We both groaned... she declaring towards the last, that the pleasure became pain. I said she had never given me so good a one. We both got into bed to have a little nap, took about an hour's doze then absolutely grubbled again and had another very good kiss. The kiss tho' not quite so good as the one before. Then another hour's nap and got up about two to undress and go regularly to bed – each took a glass of hot weak brandy and water and after my doubting a moment whether to have still another kiss we both fell asleep about three[13]'*.

---

10. 7 October 1824 – WYAS SH:7/ML/E/8/0054
11. Grubbling – penetration or stimulation with fingers
12. Kiss – Anne Lister's term for orgasm
13. 24 March 1825 – WYAS SH:7/ML/E/8/0138

As Anne journeyed farther from Mrs Barlow towards home, she mused that the relationship seemed to her *'like a dream'* and that *'this was the worst scrape*[14]*'* she had ever been in. However, back in Shibden, Anne and Mrs Barlow started corresponding, but Anne see-sawed between affection and moments of doubt towards her. Whatever her reservations, Anne was determined to see Maria Barlow again and test the relationship once more. She returned to Paris in September of 1826 with Aunt Anne and Mariana Lawton in tow. After six days in the Hôtel de la Terrasse on Rue de Rivoli, they moved into more affordable accommodation on Rue de Mondovi. Mrs Barlow was understandably distressed to see Mariana with Anne. Juggling her two lovers proved an almost impossible diplomatic feat for Anne.

Early in October as she made preparations for Mariana's return to her husband, Charles, Anne called in on Mrs Barlow to seek a favour. While Mariana waited in the street, Anne popped in to hand Mrs Barlow some money to pass on to a mutual acquaintance. *'With Mrs Barlow – she evidently pleased at Mariana's going*[15]*'* wrote Anne in her diary. On Saturday, 7 October 1826, Anne and Mariana set off from Paris to Boulogne-sur-Mer in order for Mariana to meet with Charles before they sailed home to England. The parting between Anne and

---

14. 31 March 1825 – WYAS SH:7/ML/E/8/0140
15. 6 October 1826 – WYAS SH:7/ML/E/9/0166

Mariana was difficult for her to bear. She wrote, '*I walked along the pier-side as far as I could as they passed, and Mariana waved her handkerchief as we took our last look – I went to the news-room and sat under the colonnade on one of the benches watching the vessel. My head and eyes ached, and the speck was gone beyond my sight – the sea was very rough, and as I watched the vessel heave among the breakers, my heart heaved with it, and I hope that Mariana and I would never meet to part again. Not one single tear started, but my heart was strangely heavy*[16]'.

When Anne returned to Paris a week later, she learnt that Maria Barlow had been anxiously awaiting her return. '*The porter's wife told me on entering that Mrs Barlow had called to inquire after my aunt and if I was got home almost every day – my aunt said she had never called at all – she merely wanted probably to know if I was returned*[17]'. Mrs Barlow, though still eager, was despondent. She did not like playing second fiddle to Mariana. When Anne visited, she '*found her looking the picture of despair – asked repeatedly if she was ill – no! Jane said she was not well. Said she was enough to make anyone melancholy – she would soon put me in the vapours*[18]'. The relationship was strained briefly, but soon they found common ground and in June 1827, set off for a grand tour of Switzerland

---

16. 13 October 1826 – WYAS SH:7/ML/E/9/0168
17. 14 October 1826 – WYAS SH:7/ML/E/9/0169
18. 19 October 1826 – WYAS SH:7/ML/E/9/0171

and Italy. Their choice was decided by fate, *'tossed up twice a 5-franc[19] piece. Heads to be going to Switzerland, tails remaining here – heads came up both times. Perhaps after all, we shall go'*. By the time they returned in October, Anne was certain Mrs Barlow was not the one for her. She wrote that Mrs Barlow created a *'pother'* and complained of her bad breath.

By early 1828, Anne had set up home with Madame de Rosny, a young widow with good societal connections. Despite de Rosny's intriguing life, Anne decided not to stay and left Paris to visit Sibella Maclean, who was Anne's senior by about seven years, and with whom she had cultivated a close friendship since 1820, in Scotland. Anne embarked on a tour of Scotland with Sibella during which, their relationship turned physical. However, Sibella's health had always been fragile, and when she finally had to choose between a summer in Paris with Anne, and a potential cure for her tuberculosis in London, she chose the latter.

Through her friendship with Sibella and her extended family, Anne met Sibella's niece, Vere Hobart, in 1829. Vere, in her twenties, was related to the Earl of Buckinghamshire and moved in the society circles of Baron Stuart de Rothesay and his wife, Lady Elizabeth Margaret, stylised Lady Stuart de Rothesay, the daughter

---

19. The term 'franc', first applied to a gold coin in 1360, was abbreviated from Francorum Rex, the French king's title 'King of the Franks'.

of the third Earl of Hardwicke. Vere's aristocratic credentials were irresistible and Anne began a campaign to court Vere. During Anne's journey with Vere and the Stuarts through Belgium in 1829, she recorded about thirty diary entries in crypt hand where she mused if Vere liked her. Vere proved an elusive target to Anne, but they remained friends and corresponded regularly after Vere returned to London. By May 1832, after failing to court Vere in Hastings, Anne returned home to Shibden Hall despondent that a life partner still remained beyond her reach. Ever the hopeful optimist, she turned her attentions to a neighbour, heiress Miss Ann Walker of Lidgate. She was twelve years younger and had been known to Anne since she was a teenager. Ann had always held Anne in great esteem and was a little star-struck by her confident and intelligent neighbour. By August of that year, Anne Lister was visiting Ann regularly. Ann welcomed her neighbour's attention and towards the end of 1832, they had commenced an intimate relationship. Ann's affection for Anne was undoubted, but she struggled with mental fragility. Coupled with her extreme religious faith she spiralled into the abyss of depression. Eventually, in February 1833, it was decided in Ann's best interest that she left Lidgate to live with her sister, Elizabeth, in Scotland. The lovers spent the last night together, and Ann '*said she would rather go with me. Knew she would be miserable there as she was before. Felt as if she should never come back, yet smiled and rallied when I joked her about running after me. She seemed quietly bent on being back before June when she thinks I am to be off*[20].

Ann Walker proved to be the one who had the courage to become Anne Lister's life partner. After a separation of nearly a year in 1833, they reunited. On 30 March 1834, they secretly married in the Holy Trinity Church in York by taking the sacrament together. *'The first time I ever joined Miss Walker in my prayers. I had prayed that our union might be happy*[21]*'*.

Together, they faced the disapproval of Ann's relatives and set up home in Shibden Hall. With Anne by her side, Ann Walker's confidence was reinforced. Though Ann was plagued by frequent bouts of melancholia, Anne was always there to rally her. They travelled together extensively and in 1839 embarked on what would be Anne Lister's last journey. At the age of forty-nine, on 22 September 1840, Anne died in Kutaisi, Georgia. Her remains took seven months to return home to Halifax. It travelled first by land and then by sea on a packet ship from Trebizond (modern day Trabzon in Turkey) to Gravesend in England where it arrived in April 1841.

---

20. 18 February 1833 – WYAS SH:7/ML/E/16/0018
21. 30 March 1834 – WYAS SH:7/ML/E/17/0014

Her obituary, printed on 31 October 1840 by the Halifax Guardian recognised her adventurous spirit.

> *In our obituary this week, we regret to record the name of this respected and lamented lady, whose benefactions to our charitable and religious institutions will long be remembered and whose public spirit in the improvement of our town and neighbourhood is attested by lasting memorials. In mental energy and courage she resembled Lady Mary Wortley Montagu and Lady Hester Stanhope; and like those celebrated women, after exploring Europe, she extended her reaches to those Oriental regions, where her career has been so prematurely terminated. We are informed that the remains of this distinguished lady have been embalmed and that her friend and companion, Miss Walker, is bringing them home by way of Constantinople, for interment in the family vault. She died near Tefliz but within the Circassian border. Miss Lister was descended from an ancient family in Lancashire, the main branch of which is represented by the noble line of Ribblesdale.*

On the day of her funeral, 29 April 1841, *'the road from Shibden Hall to the Parish Church was crowded, and in some places was almost impassable. On reaching the church, thousands of people were assembled to witness the sight, and it was with the greatest difficulty the corpse could be got out of the hearse*[22]*'*.

Anne Lister undoubtedly died before her time. She was always compelled to move forward into the unknown. One can only imagine how far she might have travelled, which other summits she might have conquered and what her explorations might have unearthed. However, her daring spirit lives on forever in her diaries and one should take solace in the certitude that she died doing something she loved best.

---

22. Leeds Times – Saturday, 1 May 1841

Chapter One

Serendipity

The story of Anne Lister and Ann Walker was brought to life in cinematic brilliance by Sally Wainwright, the screenwriter and producer of the BBC production, *Gentleman Jack*. The satellite dish on my roof would have been the only one on my street, and very likely in the entire neighbourhood, pointing at the United Kingdom's 28.2E Astra satellite. It now seems a strange concept in the world of online streaming.

The series provided a welcome distraction for the dire state in which Ziggy had spiralled into. Around the middle of June, I realised that it was time to let him go. His melanoma had advanced, his spondylosis and arthritis were causing him too much pain, and his chest cavity, which kept filling up with liquid, had to be drained nearly every two weeks.

I took him to Dr Waldmann for an opinion. He said it was time and that Ziggy was ready. Still, my heart overruled my mind and I could not let it happen. But the following week, after watching Ziggy for a long time, I knew I was the only one who could end his suffering. I rang Dr Waldmann's office. He said he will come to the house so we could attend to Ziggy in the privacy of my home. Dr Waldman's wife, Christina, who worked in his office made arrangements for the cremation.

They arrived late in the afternoon of Tuesday, 25 June 2019. Ziggy lay on the sofa, his head on my lap, his body still, his eyes knowing, but at peace. We said our goodbyes and as Dr Waldmann administered the injection, Christina held me.

I do not recall what I ate or drank that evening, or if I slept. I was so sad that it hurt, physically. If there was one thing I learnt about myself, it was that I grieved privately and alone. Nothing anyone could have said would have helped. They would have been redundant company. Even Chris, my long-suffering other-half who was away in Sweden, and with whom I spoke that evening, was able to provide little comfort.

The next morning, I opened the blinds to find the light had a sickly cast, as though even the sun was blighted by Ziggy's passing. Walking around the empty house was excruciating. The ache was physical. I willed myself to attend to chores and have a shower. Then I set myself the grim task of clearing a shelf in my study in preparation for Ziggy's return as a handful of ashes in an urn.

Somehow, I found distraction in the books written about Anne Lister, particularly those published by Anne Choma and Angela Steidele which provided some information about the journey Anne undertook in 1833. For want of a diversion, I sat down and plotted her journey through Germany. I live in Bonn, just an hour's drive from Koblenz, one of the towns she passed through on the way to Copenhagen. I read up about the towns and cities she had visited and the history fascinated me. I was not only intrigued by Anne Lister, but the things she found interesting captivated me too. I have visited Europe at least once every year since I was twenty-two years old. European history interests me exceedingly, be it the Middle Ages, the Hanseatic era, or World Wars I and II. I thoroughly enjoy the changing seasons, the food and drink of France, Italy, Greece, Spain and Germany, and the marvellous ancient churches and historic structures. I read Anne's diary extract of her visit to the Bleikeller in Bremen published in Anne Choma's book. Bizarrely, it filled me with a desire to look upon these very same '8 *dried bodies, dried up like leather*'. Knowing that the places Anne visited were literally at my doorstep filled me with a longing to explore. The history of these places came alive and seemed even more interesting and exciting. Even the subject of cholera in the nineteenth century seemed fascinating.

It suddenly occurred to me that at forty-two, I was the same age as Anne when she left Halifax for Copenhagen in 1833. By a strange coincidence, we shared the same initials, and at 165 centimetres and fifty-two kilogrammes, I was about the same build as Anne. The show, *Gentleman Jack*, had portrayed Anne's departure as a balm to her disappointment when Ann Walker turned down her proposal, and that she perhaps had hoped to overcome this difficult period through travel. I felt hopeful that perhaps I too could resolve my own pain through travel. After being house-bound for nearly six months, caring for Ziggy, the timing seemed perfect. Her journey was the escape I needed: to get away from a home with too many reminders of a companion I had lost, and to give me a purpose to get up every morning.

By the time the sun had set that day, I had a plan.

Anne Lister's journey in 1833

Chapter Two

Shibden to Paris

Anne Lister left Shibden Hall for her extended tour of the Continent on Sunday, 16 June 1833. She had remained in Shibden over the winter for her aunt, but now that her aunt's health was stable, business affairs at home progressing to her satisfaction and having given up hope that Ann Walker would return from Scotland, Anne was impatient to be off. She made plans to travel first to York to pick up her carriage, then to Leamington to see Mariana, and from there to London to catch up with her friends before departing for Paris. She had thought to travel towards the north, but would '*not fix beyond Paris till I get there*'.

Her departure from Shibden was without fanfare. After reading the morning prayers with her aunt, '*I soon after took my leave merely saying good morning – not contradicting the thought of my being back for a little while before winter*'. She walked just over a mile to the Stump Cross Inn to board the post coach to York, having sent her luggage ahead with her man-servant, John Booth. '*Sent John to Halifax to take care of the baggage and my place in the mail as far as the Stump Cross Inn where I meant to relieve him – sauntered along my walk all looking very pretty*'.

She arrived at the Black Swan Inn in York at quarter to six to find that her newly acquired set of servants, Thomas Beech and Eugénie Pierre, who were to accompany her to Europe, were missing. Annoyed, she finally found Thomas on Blake Street, just having set off to meet her. She had to send for Eugénie and waited for her for thirty minutes. Her servants found and sorted, she spent the next two days calling in on old friends such as the Belcombes, including Mrs Harriet Milne (Mariana's sister) and the Norcliffes. She also stopped by at the care facility where resided Eliza Raine, her childhood friend and lover who had been declared insane. She sat ten minutes with Eliza, who '*kept her eyes shut and would not speak, becoming cross so I came away. Thought her thinner in the face than when I saw her last. She is often cross and riotous – curses and swears and makes herself ill with passion and keeps the people awake all night*'.

The next day, she left York and travelled towards Leamington, via Matlock, Derby, where she was delayed fifteen minutes while waiting for sandwiches and bought several little combs, Burton upon Trent and Coleshill. Five miles from Coleshill, the hind-wheel of her carriage began to creak, producing, *'sad music on to Coleshill'*.

She had made plans to meet up with Mariana Lawton, who was in Leamington with her husband, Charles, and Mariana's niece, little Mariana. Mariana was to accompany Anne as far as London, but when they first met in Leamington, they shared just *'a very chastened kiss or two. I don't believe we either of us care much'* and Anne observed, *'no appearance of much love on either side'*. By 1833, Anne was resigned to the fact that Mariana would not leave Charles and despite being nineteen years older, it seemed more and more unlikely that he would die before the two women could be united in Shibden. Anne was now forty-two and longed for a life companion with whom she could share her quiet evenings and travel adventures. Their initial reunion was cool and strained. When she was out walking with Mariana – and perhaps in an effort to incur her jealousy – Anne told Mariana of her *'fancy for Mrs Milne'*. Mariana's reaction, or lack of one, gave Anne the impression she did not care. This moved Anne to tears. Mariana, seeming dispirited, responded with *'don't be pathetic, or you will make me so too'*.

Whatever their reservations towards each other, it did not stop them from needing the physical closeness which they found so comfortable. The next morning, Mariana went to Anne in her room where they *'had a very tolerable kiss and much talk*' and after a nice afternoon walk, they withdrew to the drawing room, and there, sufficiently out of sight of her young niece, Mariana sat on Anne's knee and she '*grubbled her well*'. They retired upstairs after tea at nine, where they '*undressed, got into bed and grubbled as before*'. Mariana was '*quite wet and nothing loth*'.

Their walks, grubbling and emotional vacillation continued during their fortnight in Leamington. They discussed the possibility of Charles's death and tossed around the options of Mariana marrying her close family friend, Willoughby Crew, or joining Anne in Shibden Hall upon his death. Mariana seemed torn between a life which conformed to societal norms and a life with Anne, and admitted '*it seems she [Mariana] did not know till now how much she cared for me*'.

However, Anne did not offer any reassurance that Shibden might still be an option for her, and when Mariana pressed her for an answer, she responded, '*I said I did not believe she knew her own mind and that I should think it not right to take any advantage of her feeling at this moment. If she remained the same a year hence, it would be another thing. Best to try the effect of absence; thus I got off fastening myself again*'.

Their situation unresolved, Anne and Mariana left Leamington on Tuesday, 2 July to travel to London. The journey took them via Gaydon in Warwick, where they changed to fresh horses. They visited St Michaels, '*the pretty hill-placed church'* of Warmington, then travelled through Banbury, which Anne noted *'one of the nicest, prettiest, neat old towns I ever saw'*. In Deddington, she remarked at *'its tall pretty spire'* before alighting at the Angel Inn in Oxford to spend the night. There, Anne *'gave her a nice little kiss by grubbling, and being near her without harm to myself'*, referring to Mariana's sexually transmitted complaint she had caught from her own philandering husband. Her discomfort included itching and resulted in a yellow-white vaginal discharge. After various nineteenth-century treatments, including the consumption of an inordinate number of grapes, and the use of vaginal douches comprised of solutions of pepper, zinc sulphate and mercury, Anne had managed to control her condition. She had learned not to *'be near'* (vulva to vulva contact) with Mariana in order to successfully avoid a repeat of her infection.

The next afternoon, they resumed their journey, passing West Wycombe, with its *'most striking church on the hill'* and *'Sir John Dashwood-King's (Baronet) handsome place and grounds below'*. They passed the *'neat, picturesque little town'* of Beaconsfield at twenty past six in the evening, and at Uxbridge, they alighted at the Crown Inn briefly to view *'the room in which Charles I held a treaty with his parliament in 1643-4. Document and signatures framed and hanged over the chimney piece'*. They then continued their journey to London and *'alighted at Hawkins's, 26 Dover Street, London'*, at thirty-five minutes past nine in the evening and sat down to tea, ham and eggs.

At Hawkins's, Anne found that Vere Hobart, now Lady Vere Cameron since her marriage to Donald Cameron of Lochiel in July 1832, had called at the hotel and left her card. She had been heavily pregnant when she stopped by and early the next morning Anne received news that Vere had given birth to a girl whom she later named Anne Louisa Cameron.

Anne spent a further fortnight in London, catching up with her old friends Lady Stuart, Lady Stuart de Rothesay, Lady Caroline Duff Gordon and Lady Vere Cameron. She was introduced to Miss Tate, '*an elderly maiden lady, very plain, neither much mannerism nor haut ton*[1], *but very musical (plays well and had the remains of a good voice and manner of singing) and apparently very good. Must have a good fortune to have her house and live so well in London and, besides, her place Langdown near Southampton. Evidently an useful friend of Lady Stuart's, otherwise not a person whose rank or manners would get her into Lady Stuart's society*'.

She continued making preparations for her journey, having her will lodged at Hammersley's one of the chief bankers in London in the nineteenth century, alongside Coutts, and Messrs Herries, Farquhar & Co.

---

1. The haut ton were the fashionable elite of society. They exhibited the refined manners which characterised those of good breeding and fortune.

She went shopping at Cheapside and bought a pair of blue spectacles and a small compass. She arranged for her manservant, Thomas, to have some new clothes at a cost of £20, equal to about £2,340 in 2020. She went to Stammer's in the Strand, Rundle and Bridges, and Thomas's, on the corner of Bond and Bruton Streets where she spent a considerable time sourcing and deciding upon a coffee-pot set for Vere. She finally chose the set and a lamp at Thomas's. This decision cost her £39 and eighteen shillings, equivalent to about £4,700 today. Her budget of £20 blown, Anne regretted her decision to continue to ingratiate herself with Vere, writing, '*this second-hand concern came to about forty pounds. I could have one better at Rundle Bridges. Vexed at heart but said nothing even to Mariana. May I manage better another time. Mind how I make promises*'.

While Anne had a whirlwind of social commitments in London, Mariana was left behind to languish in their hotel or in the carriage waiting for her. At one point, frustrated and neglected, Mariana broke down. Anne recalled, '*poor Mariana on hearing I was going to dine out, burst into tears. She had been counting the minutes for me and this unexpected disappointment made her quite nervous. She felt alone and bitterly repented having come with me. I was courted, she neglected and unknown, and now our unsuitableness seemed to strike her forcibly*'. Anne softened, and even though she did attend dinner at Miss Tate's, she cut her visit short. '*Miss Tate's carriage came for me at 7 – only herself, Lady Stuart and me. Lady Stuart had ordered her carriage for me at 11. I said Mrs Lawton was with me and not well and had the carriage and was at home at 9 20/.. under other circumstances should have been sorry not to have staid longer for today, as yesterday, spent a pleasant evening. Lady Stuart very kind – Miss Tate all anxious to please and therefore very civil and attentive to me. An unexpected pleasure to Mariana to have me back so soon'.*

Back with Mariana, they had tea together and retired at half past eleven, with Anne concluding her diary of 5 July 1833 with *'Mariana very nervous but I did all I could to comfort and set her at ease. Very fine day – F67° at 12 20/.. tonight'*. It seems that Mariana was set at her ease by physical closeness, as Anne recorded in her diary first thing the next day, writing, *'grubbled a little last night. Mariana's eyes swelled up this morning with her crying of yesterday'*. Mariana once again sought assurance from Anne, but this time, Anne divulged how years of waiting for Mariana had affected her. *'Convinced Mariana I had more common sense than she thought and valued my own happiness above all other things. Could give up the world any day. Few people valued it less than I did but as to Mariana, said she had shaken my confidence and it would now require some effort on her part to renew it, but as Milton had said, we forgave soonest those we had loved longest. However, I did not make any promises'.*

A few days later, when Anne was scheduled to meet her *haut ton* friends at the National Gallery, Mariana suggested trailing along secretly to satisfy her curiosity of Anne's friends. '*Mariana anxious to see them all without being known. Took Watson[2] and went, agreeing that we were not to take any notice of each other. She was close to us several times. She told me afterwards the seeing me in that way made her feel queer and sick. I said it was queer enough to me, but the fact was I neither cared nor thought about it*'. Anne's bravado only covered up her private insecurities, '*I too had my hidden mortification. I am always fancying I have done some gaucherie[3] or that people see my stiffness and unfitness for the world, etc. etc.*'.

Anne's insecurities aside, she appeared to have made a good impression on Miss Tate, recording that '*she said I reminded her of her father who used to say the world was like a stage coach. If one was not ready to go with it, one must be left behind. She said how many would be glad of me for a companion*'. However when she mentioned her plans to explore the Urals, Lady Stuart and Miss Tate were anxious for her safety, and advised her '*against my doing more than Saint Petersburg and Moscow (I had talked of an excursion to the Ural Mountains). It would be odd and talked of*'.

Finally, at twenty to two on Wednesday afternoon, 18 July 1833, Anne left London to travel to Paris. She passed Shooter's Hill and Dartford and arrived at Canterbury

---

2. Watson was Mariana Lawton's servant

3. gaucherie (French): awkwardness, to do something embarrassing

at quarter to eleven. She considered staying the night, but '*took fright at the little pokey sitting room*' and ordered a new set of horses and headed off. She arrived at Wright's Hotel in Dover at one o'clock in the morning, immediately had tea and ham and retired to her room an hour later. She was in a pensive mood and wrote in her diary, '*reflective. Did not read but very fairly happy today and castle building about writing, publishing and making my book pay my expenses*'.

Several hours later, she breakfasted at quarter to nine and then boarded the Ferret packet service, at 140 tonnes, a '*fine, fast vessel*' in the charge of Captain John Hamilton. To the delight of Anne, who was prone to bouts of seasickness, the passage was calm. '*Nobody sick. I sat or rather lay in my carriage half asleep all the way. Smooth water yet a fine cool pleasant air blowing thro' all my open windows*'. She landed in Calais after nearly two and a half hours since weighing anchor and settled into l'Hôtel Quillacq, and set to writing to her aunt. '*You know I have long wished to see Trèves, and the valley of the Moselle. I think of doing this, and getting out upon Coblentz, and so seeing a little of Germany – but you shall hear more of it from Paris*'. Then she wrote to Mariana of her good sea crossing and '*bade her take care of herself. Ride, walk, read and do all she could to be well and happy. I had always a presentment that all would be well at last, and never despaired*'.

Anne set off early from Calais the next morning at half past four. Her carriage trundled through Ardres, La Recousse and Saint-Omer which she described as a *'large, dull town'* but with the saving grace of a handsome cathedral with *'one of the handsomest looking organs (at west end) I ever saw'*.

From Saint-Omer, she jolted along in her carriage on a hard and unforgiving pavé[4] road through Aire-sur-la-Lys, Lillers, a *'goodish little town,'* and then to Pernes. At Saint-Pol-sur-Ternoise she let her servants sit down to dinner in the kitchen of the hotel while she grabbed half a roll and sauntered about the town and visited the church. In thirty minutes, they were on their way again, rumbling through Frévent and arriving at Amiens to stop for the night at Hôtel de la Poste.

Anne awoke at five past nine on the Saturday morning, 20 July, recorded the temperature in her bedroom at *'67°F at 10 ¼ a.m. in my bedroom, no sun'* and breakfasted at twenty past ten. Then she headed out and sought out Amiens Cathedral, thinking it a *'very fine cathedral. Finest I have seen in France – no white wash – the natural stone, and very neat, and clean, and as little unencumbered as a Roman Catholic place of worship can be. Tho' some very fine altars in the chapels and two in the transept. High altar, handsome – backed by fine apsis. Fine carved scripture histories on the outside of the chancel side-screen, and a few*

---

4. *pavé* (French): road paved with stone

elsewhere, in very high relief. Fine, painted glass windows in the transept – light but close screen between the chancel and transept. The only church to be named with York'. Anne had a tendency to compare most of the churches she saw to the York Minster – and rightly so. York Minster is spectacular and one of the largest churches in Northern Europe. The Amiens Cathedral though, stands loftily and distinctly in the skyline of Amiens, the capital of ancient Picardy. Approaching it in the nineteenth century, prior to the construction of modern buildings, would have rendered the view extraordinary. Amiens also had another historical significance; it was here in 1802 that the Treaty of Amiens was signed, signifying the end of the French Revolutionary Wars between Great Britain and France, until the start of the Napoleonic Wars the following year. Anne *'peeped into the Palais de Justice (the court arcaded round like a cloister) and walked thro' the halle au bled*[5]*'* and came to the conclusion, *'Amiens a nice, good town – handsome wide streets. One might live there or in the neighbourhood well enough'*.

From Amiens, she made her way to Chantilly, the towns of Hébécourt, Flers-sur-Noye, Breteuil, Saint-Just-en-Chaussée, Wavignies, Clermont and Laigneville forming an idyllic French collage of traditional country life, observing *'people weaving black bourre de soie (spun silk) stockings'* and the *'striking and picturesque'* landscape. At

---

5. *Halle au Bled* (French): Corn market, grain exchange

Shibden to Paris

Chantilly, she alighted at the Hôtel d'Angleterre at nine-thirty in the evening and arranged for accommodation for herself and her servants.

> *Some time bargaining for apartment 5/. and servants eating and my own (everything compris[6] but wax lights for myself) 12/. par jour[7] = 17 francs a day. Had boiled milk and bread and butter at 10. Excellent bread. Had Thomas up – asked if he had had anything to eat. 'Yes! Thank you, ma'am, I have had a good supper, thank God for it'. Poor fellow! His gratitude upon the occasion amused me exceedingly. Very fine day – but a little rain this evening, a few drops. F68 ½° now at 11 p.m.*
>
> – 20 July 1833

Anne paused her journey in Chantilly for four days, taking the time to bring her journal up to date. As always, the process of writing her thoughts down gladdened her.

> *Heartily glad to get straight again with my journal. The writing, which is somehow always a comfort to me, however triste[8], turning to it always does me good. I had many reflections as I came along on Friday and Saturday. Solitude seemed to me very*

---

6. *compris* (French): inclusive
7. *par jour* (French): per day
8. *triste* (French): sad

fearful but my journal has reconciled me very much.
– 22 July 1833

Home to the famed silk lace, *blonde* and luscious cream, the city of Chantilly, forty-two kilometres north of Paris, was also the site of Château de Chantilly, an impressive, sprawling estate to which Louis de Bourbon, the Prince of Condé, famed for his military campaign successes, retired. In his later life, he surrounded himself with literary geniuses such as Racine, Molière and Bossuet – men whom Anne had read and respected. It was here in 1659 that Molière's satire, *Les Précieuses Ridicules* was first performed. Condé took great pride in the beautiful château and great pleasure in entertaining. In 1671, in political reconciliation to Louis XIV, he hosted a party of three days and three nights. About four thousand people needed feeding in the most luxurious fashion. His talented chef, François Vatel, who had spent the past twelve sleepless nights stressing about the preparations, lost his head in despair when the fish he ordered from the ports of Haute-Normandie did not arrive in time. Vatel, at forty years of age, committed suicide by wedging his sword against a door and throwing himself on it. The fish finally did arrive, but Louis XIV and the guests refrained from eating the fish out of respect for Vatel.

The Château de Chantilly was destroyed during the French Revolution during the late eighteenth century. When Anne visited all that remained were Condé's petit château and the expansive stables that were capable of housing over two hundred horses. Arbele poplars had taken root in the ruins of the main château. Ironically, Anne noted that the canals that ran alongside Chantilly were full of fish.

> *Took a little girl from there as guide thro' the gardens and to the palace and écuries,[9] the Jardin Anglais of the last 13 years' creation very pretty but all the trees of the fir tribe. L'isle d'amour nothing, a mere road to and thro' a sort of large charpente[10] (wood painted white). Covered walk thro' two straight narrowish canals but full of fish. The grand canal (½ lieue[11] long) fine. Not much to see in the palace or château – handsome gallery – the battles of the great Condé on each side of it. These were sequestrated in the First Revolution when the Grand Château was demolished, but picked up again and repurchased by the last Duc de Bourbon.*
>
> *In the Château d'Enghien (called by the late Duc, poor d'Enghien's father, Château Neuf because he could not bear to hear it called by his son's name) at a*

---

9. *écuries* (French): stables
10. *charpente* (French): gateway
11. *lieue* (French): historical reference to league (distance). In 1833, the metric *lieue* was used in France, with 1 metric *lieue* being about 2.5 miles (4 km).

> *little distance above the château a good plain range of building, nothing particular to see, so did not go to it – the écuries 600 feet long for 180 horses (when the troops were quartered there, there were 400 horses). Magnificent.*
>
> *– 23 July 1833*

At the stables, Anne ascended to the level above where the servants lodged. The apartments opened into a balcony which provided views of Mortefontaine to the south-east, the easterly forests of Ermenonville, and '*Senlis Cathedral (4 petites lieues distant) very conspicuous*'. This may have brought back memories of a time she spent with Maria Barlow in Mortefontaine and Senlis. It was a sultry May in 1827 and Anne had arranged for an excursion to Mortefontaine, Ermenonville and Senlis for herself, Mrs Barlow and her daughter, Jane. In Mortefontaine, during a moment of jealous passion partly fuelled by wine, Mrs Barlow snatched the locket Mariana had given Anne from her neck.

> *The little ring that held the string gave way and down fell the locket. 'What the devil did you do that for? Damn it, you need not have done that!'*
>
> *She sought for and picked up the locket and got into bed. I stood a long while pressing the ring close and re-putting thro' it the string. Obliged to untie the knot poor Mariana had tied when she gave it me. I*

put the whole in my purse for the night and got into bed full of reflection. Jane had asked what was the matter. 'Nothing', said Mrs Barlow, and Jane wisely said no more.

I never uttered but being annoyed and feverish, passed a very restless night. Thought I, perhaps it is for the best. It is a good excuse for my having nothing to say to her, and I am glad to be off. I will take care how I put myself in this situation again. In the middle of the night she whispered me to kiss and forgive her. I kissed her coldly – awoke at five and a quarter. Going to get up – Mrs Barlow began talking, hoped she had done the locket no harm. Did not mean to do that; only could not bear me to sleep in it. Told her a word would have done. I would have taken it off. She had no need to do as she did and had annoyed me exceedingly. She began talking about whether I loved her best. At last she teased me till after a long and persevering silence, I said yes. She seemed half distracted (all in a smothered way for fear Jane should not be asleep).

A great deal of nonsense. I wished myself anywhere but here. I was, and silently promised myself, to excursionize with her no more. However, it ended as usual in right middle finger up. Could not give her a best excitement for fear of Jane. Did not give her

> *the feel of a kiss but pretended I had had one (was in fact a little excited) – afterwards dozed. I wonder if Jane was awake. Mrs Barlow pinned our curtains together that she could not see much but might hear moving about.*
>
> *– 3 May 1827*

Anne may have faked her orgasm in Mortefontaine, but by the time they were in Senlis, the locket incident was not as raw, and Anne had fallen once again under the lascivious charms of Mrs Barlow.

> *Last night right middle finger up (Jane the next room to us) and two kisses. At it again from six and a half this morning to getting up with dozing between. Middle finger up and three kisses then playing. She on my left thigh but tho' as near her as yesterday, had not at all a kiss to myself nor had she a right that is a best one, tho' she said she felt for me the whole time I was handling her or near her.*
>
> *I this morning looked at her, kissed the top hair with my mouth and letting fall a little saliva. This excited her again. The bed both yesterday and this morning was a good deal wet. My night things and hair wet through. Would not curl at all. I have hardish work with her. I should have got up early yesterday and today but she kept me in bed. She has certainly passion enough for me.*
>
> *– 6 May 1827*

Whatever memories might have run through Anne's mind, as she stood on the balcony of the servants' quarters taking in the view, she did not allude to them in her diary of 1833. From the stables, Anne walked the five kilometres to the Château de la Reine Blanche, a distance she covered in a little over an hour '*at the rate of good 3 miles per hour*', a pace which not only tired out her servants, Eugénie and Thomas, but later earned her a run in her stocking and a blistered right foot. The château, flanked by four towers at the corners, is situated in the midst of the Chantilly forest. The '*very pretty little Gothic building*', was named after Blanche of Castile, mother to Louis IX. She was said to have lived there but the château, built in 1293 by the Lord of Viarmes, was not yet in existence during her lifetime. When Anne visited in 1833, the château would have been relatively newly restored. The works were carried out by Louis VI Henri de Bourbon-Condé between 1826 and 1828 to convert the building into a hunting lodge. Bourbon-Condé did not get long to enjoy the lodge and died at the age of seventy-four just two years later. The building is now used as a private function facility for weddings, baptisms, and birthdays.

The death of Bourbon-Condé was a subject of great speculation; he was found strangled with a double handkerchief tied with an adjut knot in August 1830. Claims abound of a murder or assassination disguised as a suicide, but it was also speculated that his death was caused while engaging in autoerotic asphyxiation with his mistress, British courtesan Sophie Dawes. Dawes was born to a fisherman and smuggler from the Isle of Wight and met Bourbon-Condé while working as a courtesan in London. At age nineteen, she became his mistress. Dawes later married General-Baron Adrien Victor de Feuchères and was stylised Baroness de Feuchères, though she remained Bourbon-Condé's mistress without her husband's knowledge. The situation surrounding Baroness de Feuchères and Bourbon-Condé's death was still a topic of gossip in 1833. Anne remarked that *'it seems Madame de Feuchères is not at all liked here – they all think because she was not a French woman, she murdered the poor prince. But my landlady herself thinks that human nature could not surely be guilty of such scélératesse*[12] *– they all think the king wrong to notice her so much'*.

After the intensive sightseeing of the previous days, or perhaps to tend to her blister, Anne spent 24 July at her apartment in Hôtel d'Angleterre writing out her travelling accounts and reading Le Constitutionnel, a French trade, political and literary daily. She noted, *'the cholera now bad at Rotterdam, and has appeared again at Antwerp'*. By August 1833, daily deaths as a result of cholera in Antwerp and Rotterdam peaked at 120 a day[13].

---

12. *scélératesse* (French): villainy
13. *A Monthly Magazine of Interesting and Instructive Science and Literature*, published January 1841.

It was not until 1854 that contaminated drinking water was proven to be the source of the disease.

Anne found her accommodation at Chantilly *'very snug and comfortable'* and was *'very well satisfied'* but decided it was time to move on to Paris. They packed up the next day and travelled through *'very pretty undulating, richly wooded country all about Chantilly – nice drive all the way to Paris'*. At Écouen, she took an hour to visit the Château d'Écouen, built in the reign of Francis I in the sixteenth century.

> *Nothing but bare walls – the Duc[14] de Bourbon has left it and 5000 per annum to found a college. In the time of Napoleon, it was a school for 500 mademoiselles de la légion d'honneur (i.e. daughters, sisters, nieces or cousins of the chevaliers[15]). It was démantelé[16] in the First Revolution – frescos, paintings, marbles, etc. destroyed. The famous vitres peintes[17] the history of Psyche par Raffael du temps du Connétable[18] Anne de Montmorency (whose 4 pelicans (his arms) are still left on some of the walls, and on the Dutch tile pavement of one or two rooms)*

---

14. *duc* (French): duke
15. *chevaliers* (French): knights
16. *démantelé* (French): demolished
17. *vitres peintes* (French): stained glass, painted glass windows
18. *par Raffael du temps du Connétable...* (French): by Raffael in the time of Constable...

> *were cassées[19], but the remains of them were collected by the Duke de Bourbon and sent to Chantilly.*
>
> – 25 July 1833

Château d'Écouen has been home to the collections of the National Museum of the Renaissance since 1975. While most of the original stained glass was removed in the eighteenth and nineteenth centuries, it still exhibits an impressive collection of stained glass, amongst other *objet d'arts*. Some of the original stained glass from Château d'Écouen referred to by Anne is displayed at the Château of Chantilly, even today.

On resuming her journey into Paris, Anne encountered no troubles at the customs barrier in Clichy, '*a douanier[20] merely looked in and civilly asked if I had anything that should pay duty, and on my saying 'no', let the carriage drive on*'. Arriving into Paris just before three in the afternoon, she checked into the Hôtel de la Terrasse on Rue de Rivoli and set about arranging for their catering for the week. Then with Eugénie she walked to her little apartment at 27 Rue St Victor. She had retained the apartment for an annual rent of £17 (a value of about £2,000 in 2020) when she left Paris in May 1831. Entering her apartment, she was disappointed to find her books, '*sadly dusty*'.

---

19. *cassées* (French): broken
20. *douanier* (French): customs officer

She was also very aware that her old flame, Maria Barlow was still waiting in the wings. Their time apart had not made the situation any clearer, and Anne was now disillusioned with Mariana. During their time together in Leamington and London, Mariana had repeatedly tried to obtain Anne's assurance that, if Charles Lawton died, Anne would welcome her permanently into Shibden. Anne was also painfully aware that Mrs Barlow lacked *éclat*[21] and wealth. With all that on her mind, Anne mused, '*I am not quite determined what to do about Mrs Barlow, but feel very composed about it*'.

But the odds were stacked against poor Mrs Barlow.

---

21. *éclat* (French): style, class, polished in mannerisms

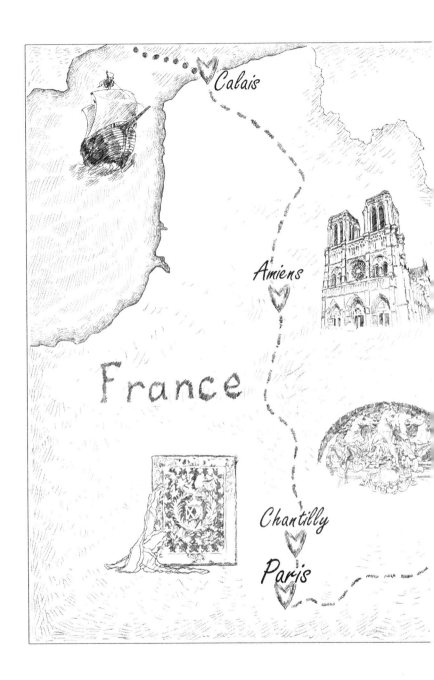

Anne Lister's route from Calais to Luxembourg in 1833

Chapter Three

Paris to Luxembourg

Paris in July 1833 was a bustling city and still growing. The trauma of the July Revolution of 1830 was almost behind it, and Louis-Philippe I had been elected by parliament to be king. He was a liberal constitutional monarch popular with the wealthy bourgeoisie, and during his early rule, took action to develop broad-based reforms to benefit the people. He stylised himself the 'King of the French', instead of 'King of France'. However, he was not popular with the Republicans and the Legitimists who considered Charles X's young grandson, Henri d'Artois the rightful heir to the throne. In addition, Louis-Philippe I was resented by the poorer classes who felt that he mainly supported the interests of the wealthy.

By the early 1830s, the accelerating French Industrial Revolution had enticed a large influx of workers to Paris, which swelled housing capacity in the old neighbourhoods to its limits. Poor water quality and sanitation made the areas around the Notre-Dame Cathedral and Tuileries a prime breeding ground for cholera. In March 1832, the first cases of cholera appeared in the city. Paris's Hôtel-Dieu, on the Île de la Cité, was inundated with what seemed like the living dead. In a matter of days, the victims of cholera were transformed from what was human into a grotesquely deformed shape, devastated by extreme stomach cramps, and with countenances turned into livid-blue masks with dark, hollow eyes. An observer of the time wrote, *'the sick person is overtaken simultaneously by vertigo, retching, and diarrhoea, painful cramps in the limbs, and a sudden coldness of the body, which soon assumes a cadaverous look, resulting especially from the deep hollowing of the eyes and from the frightful alteration of the features. The pulse slows down... and disappears within a few hours... The nails and fingertips turn a blue colour, which gradually spreads to the lips, the area around the eyes, and, with varied nuances, on the whole surface of the body... Breathing is short, quick, panting, breath is cold; and all these symptoms of suffocation conclude with the extinction of life*'[1].

---

1. Joseph-Claude-Anthelme Récamier, de l'Académie Royale de Médecine – *Recherches sur le traitement du choléra morbus* (Paris, 1832)

In Paris, the cholera epidemic of 1832 was contained by late September, but at a cost of nearly twenty thousand Parisian lives. The people of Paris blamed the government, and the rich fled the city. As the disease continued to ravage those unable to escape the city and in areas of poor sanitation, cholera became known as the disease of the poor. The bourgeoisie blamed the poor working class for the disease, and the poor accused the rich of poisoning them. The tense climate combined with Louis-Philippe's poor handling of the crisis made him unpopular, a point not lost to Anne who recorded in her diary on 28 July 1833, that she '*had seen the king and his cortège pass. Very few vivas – our George IV would have had as many when his popularity was at the lowest. Seems a fearfully general impression that the king will be shot at today*' and later that day, in a letter to her aunt, noted '*a strangely general impression that a certain high personage is to be shot at in the procession. Throughout all the world how little men's minds seem settled! But no more – never write politics. I have thought of you, my dear aunt, perpetually, and feel very odd without you here*'.

The political turmoil of France set aside, Anne turned her attention to more pressing matters. She knew she could not put off Mrs Barlow any longer and called on her at her apartment in 4 Rue Neuve du Luxembourg. Anne was determined to play her cards right this time, and '*sat an hour with Mrs Barlow. All as usual but no kissing or allusion to anything particular. All very good friends*'.

The next day she called on Mrs Barlow again and visited for nearly an hour. This visit did not end quite so well, with Anne privately thinking, '*Mrs Barlow now seems to me almost vulgar, to say the least of it. Talks as greatly as she can of Italy. I am determined not to be seen in the streets with her*'. However, for one trying not to be associated with Mrs Barlow, Anne inexplicably rented the third floor of the same building Mrs Barlow was residing in; perhaps the rent of fifty shillings a week, far cheaper than what she was paying at the Hôtel de la Terrasse sweetened the deal.

While with Mrs Barlow, Anne was forwarded a letter through the embassy from Lady Stuart, who wrote, '*I trust to hear from you, dear Miss Lister, as you can leave no friend more interested about you*'. Lady Stuart's kind letter touched Anne, and she realised, '*she is really kind, worth them all and a hundred of Vere into the bargain*'.

Anne resettled into life in Paris and prepared for her onward journey. Her little apartment on Rue St Victor needed tidying, and she had to decide if she wanted to keep the apartment or let it go, and if she should re-home her collection of books. She had social calls to attend to, and needed to plan her route, remarking '*I still think of the north – one of its accommodations is that it is cheaper than the south*' and thought, '*of going by Rheims, Verdun, Luxembourg, Trèves, Coblentz, Cassel, etc. etc.*'.

Four days after arriving in Paris, Anne visited her old acquaintance, Countess Maria Assunta Butini de

Bourke, sixty-nine years of age, and widow of Count Edmund de Bourke. Madame de Bourke was well regarded by society despite her mysterious period of life in Naples where she had met Edmund de Bourke. He was then a Danish diplomat and appointed to the court of Naples as minister, and he had a reputation for liking the casinos and the trappings that came with it. In 1783, he had inherited a large fortune from his father, who was a plantation owner in St Croix, then part of the Danish West Indies. It was rumoured that he married her out of gratitude when she paid off a gambling debt that he was unable to settle quickly enough. Whatever their reasons, they made a charming couple and, in 1820, moved to Paris where de Bourke's diplomatic role was transferred. When Count de Bourke passed away at the baths of Vichy in August 1821 after an extended illness, he left his inconsolable widow with a noble title and a fortune that allowed her to remain comfortably in Paris.

Madame de Bourke was delighted to see Anne again and the timing was perfect. Her niece Sophie Ferral was to travel to Copenhagen and Madame de Bourke asked if Anne would let the young Miss Ferral accompany her. Anne was open to having a travel companion but made it clear that her plans involved an indirect route to Copenhagen.

> *Agreed to take her. She, of course, to pay all her own expense. Said I was not going there direct. Heard all*

> *the story of her refusing a Russian with two thousand sterling a year but twenty years older than herself. The young lady twenty-four. Madame de Bourke determined to get rid of her.*
>
> *I promised never to tell all she had told me, and she not to say to the girl herself she had told me. When at last I rather fought off, she said it would be a kindness, a charity and I agreed. How extraordinary, thought I. Well, I am at any rate companioned.*
>
> – 30 July 1833

Madame de Bourke and Anne made plans to meet again so that she may meet Sophie Ferral. Several days later, Madame de Bourke and Miss Ferral dropped in at Anne's apartment at 4 Rue Neuve du Luxembourg. The climb up to the third floor proved an exertion too great for the elderly Madame de Bourke. Anne observed, '*poor Madame de Bourke half dead with coming upstairs*'. Upon meeting Miss Ferral, '*a nice, pretty looking girl,*' Anne '*wondered how we shall get on together and whether it is for good or not that I shall have her*'.

While in Paris, Anne also met the 31-year-old John Lister, the son of John Lister of Swansea, Wales, who would eventually come to inherit Shibden at Anne's death. Anne gave him some solid advice. '*Advised his not thinking of trying for the infirmary at Swansea and settling there as surgeon and apothecary. No graduating with credit afterwards and a Glasgow diploma worth nothing. Better toil on – make a sacrifice to graduate at Edinburgh. Keep in sight of the friends he has made in the company's service, and hope and try for something by and by'.*

She also called on her old learned circle mostly from her time at le Jardin des Plantes, René Louiche Desfontaines, who lectured botany, Étienne Geoffroy Saint-Hilaire, the French zoologist, Alexandre Brongniart, mineralogist, Mr Juilliart, and the widow of Georges Cuvier (Madame Cuvier), and her daughter, Sophie Duvaucel.

When she called at Desfontaines's, he, then eighty-three, was '*quite blind, and very feeble*'. He was nonetheless glad for her visit, and Anne presented him with, '*one of my Rodgers[2] four-blade mother-of-pearl penknives with which (with the attention) he seemed flattered and pleased*'.

Anne had studied anatomy and palaeontology under Georges Cuvier during her time in Paris, in the winter between 1829 and 1830. He had died in May 1832, at the age of sixty-two, a victim of the dreaded cholera. Anne, out of respect to her old lecturer, called on his widow, Anne-Marie. Her daughter, Sophie, was Cuvier's former assistant, and a scientific illustrator. When they met, Cuvier's widow and stepdaughter were '*very civil and glad to see me – gave me the éloge[3] on Mr Cuvier, and some*

---

2. Rodgers of Sheffield was established in the eighteenth century and was appointed cutlers to the British royal family in 1821. Anne misspelt the establishment frequently in her diary as 'Rogers'.

3. *éloge* (French): eulogy

of his last brochures. Said I was only here for ten days, but hoped to see them again'.

She gifted Juilliart four scalpels, one of them from Rodgers Sheffield, and sent two razors to Geoffroy Saint-Hilaire, who was unfortunately *'in the country this fortnight and would not be back of eight days'*.

In between her social calls, she continued to see Maria Barlow and wrote letters home especially to Mariana Lawton, from whom she sought the recipe for Four Thieves Vinegar. During the plague epidemic in the eighteenth century, Four Thieves Vinegar was hailed as a preventive measure against the plague disease. One version of the recipe, published in 1770, states:

> *Take of rue, wormwood, sage, lavender, mint and rosemary, of each one handful; put them altogether, with a gallon of the best vinegar, into a stone-pan; covered over with paste, and let them stand within the warmth of a fire to infuse for eight days; then strain them off, and to every quart bottle put three quarters of an ounce of camphire*[4]*. Let the camphire be dissolved before it is put into bottles. Rub the temples and loins with this preparation before*

---

4. Camphor, henna flower (or plant)

going out in a morning, wash the mouth, and snuff up some of it into the nostrils, and carry a piece of sponge, that has been dipped in it, in order to smell it pretty often[5].

It is uncertain what Anne Lister was expecting to encounter in her journey through Germany to Copenhagen, but perhaps she felt that rubbing her temple and loins in vinegar and herbs might well prevent any infectious disease. At any rate, there is neither evidence that Mariana provided the recipe, nor that she might have used this frightful concoction.

Finally, it was time for her to leave Paris and the days leading up to her departure saw a flurry of activity. Final tweaks to her carriage were carried out. She ordered six pairs of black gloves and eight pairs each of white, light grey and darker from Privat's. Her watch was repaired and serviced by the famous watchmaker, Perrelet & Fils, at 108 Rue Saint Honoré. She studied Heinrich Reichard's itinerary for travel through Germany, and determined upon travelling '*via Luxembourg, Trêves, Coblentz, Cassel, Hanover, Hamburg and Lubeck*'. She stored sixteen bottles of wine in her cellar at Rue St Victor and arranged for her books in the apartment to be wrapped up in paper to protect them, and left there under the care of Mr Audouin.

---

5. Newcastle Courant – Saturday, 20 October 1770

A quick note to the Secretary of Legation, Arthur Aston Esquire of the British Embassy, arranged for passports for both Sophie Ferral and herself. She wrote, *'Miss Lister presents her compliments to Mr Aston and will be much obliged to him if he will be so good as to arrange her passport for Madame Lister to travel in Germany and the north of Europe; and if he will also be so good as insert the name of her friend Mademoiselle Sophie Ferral – 4 August, 4 Rue Neuve du Luxembourg'.*

She wrote a frenzy of letters to family and friends, and gave instructions to her land steward, Samuel Washington via her aunt:

> *To give £120 per acre for Mrs Walsh's land if she and her son would join to give the best security they could. The money to be advanced by Washington and what interest right charged till the next rent and then the money to be taken out of the rents. If the Misses Walker do not come to an agreement, sign the one drawn up in a fortnight from Mr Parker's writing to them again. An action to be commenced to get written deposition from Timothy Spaight about the Lower Brea water and may get counsel's opinion but wish to be as quiet in the matter as I can during old Wilkinson's life.*
>
> – 18 August 1833

To Lady Stuart she wrote:

I feel as if I should get on very well – the greatest puzzle I have is ordering dinner... this solitary journey may do me good. It will shew me how far I may really trust to the resources of my own mind. From the moment they fail me, or threaten to do so, I shall date my return. Ever dearest Lady Stuart, very affectionately yours, Anne Lister.

– 29 July 1833

She addressed Mariana:

Never make yourself uneasy about me. You have learnt that I am not fickle as the summer's wind, and that I have believe it possible to make new friends without losing old ones. I hope my heart is at any rate better than my head, and that it has been those who have known me least who have done me most injustice.

God bless you, Mary! I am not perhaps so easily spoilt as you imagine. As to the kindness of my friends in London or elsewhere, I am not conscious that it has ever done other than make me more anxious to deserve it. I shall think of you often, particularly in Germany where music is so frequent and so fine.

Again and again God bless you! Tell me every now and then that my absence has less and less of its former bad effects, and believe me, my love ever entirely and very especially yours, Anne Lister.

– 2 August 1833

Throughout her stay in Paris, Anne had been in receipt of letters from home but the one that affected her most was received from Elizabeth Sutherland, Ann Walker's sister, who had written from Udale, Fortrose in Scotland. Ann had left Lidgate in February to stay with her sister, Elizabeth, for the sake of her health. *'Mrs Sutherland perplexed about her sister – better in bodily health, at least fatter, but still (it seems?) no better in spirits'*. Mrs Sutherland's letter stated, *'I am aware from what my sister has repeatedly stated that there is no individual living by whom she would be so much influenced, and my only consolation is that thro' your kind interference and influence she may be directed to do that which will promote her happiness as at present she is certainly unable to judge for herself. Anxiously expecting to hear from you and where I can address you with a certainty of my letter reaching you'*.

The letter obviously played on Anne's mind, and she reminisced as she was prone to do. For the first time since leaving Shibden on 16 June, Anne *'incurred a cross[6] just before getting up, thinking of Miss Walker'*. Then, after breakfast, she sat down and responded to Mrs Sutherland's letter.

---

6. incurred a cross: Anne's own term for masturbation

My dear Mrs Sutherland,

I received your letter yesterday, and lose no time in answering it, and in expressing my very sincere regret that your sister's health is not more entirely re-established. I hope your not having written more explicitly, is unimportant; as I have so long contemplated the possible or probable circumstances of the case, that I am perhaps already nearly as well acquainted with it, as you can desire. I was aware when your sister left home, that something more than a mere visit to you was necessary; and that you must discover this sooner or later. I was aware also, that Lidgate was not the place where she ought to be left alone; and she will remember with what earnestness I represented this to her, again and again. I entreat you to shew her this letter, and say, if my influence is still unshaken, I am sure that, with your approbation and under your direction, she will follow my advice. I shall give it without reserve, as the best means in my power of proving how much I am really interested for her. It is, in the first place, necessary to ascertain the real state of morbid disturbance under which the mind is labouring. I have not mentioned my own opinion on this subject, to anyone, but your aunt, Miss Walker, just before my leaving home, and Dr Belcombe in whose secrecy, and honour, I have as much confidence, as in his experience, and skill in this particular branch of medical practice. I strongly recommend your writing to him to take your sister under his care, to provide a proper person to be with her, and a lodging, and every comfort, and everything cheerful. You need be under no apprehension – you may safely leave all to him. He is too well accustomed to this sort of thing, and will do his utmost for his own sake, as well as for mine, as he knows how much I feel interested. You will mention your wish that the thing should not be known. Your sister can take any name she likes for the time; and you can so manage both friends and business for her, in the interim, that no one needs know she is not still with you. I have always told her everything plainly and without the least concealment. I have even, in some sort, suggested this plan to her before. Do give my love, and tell her, that if she will only consent to do what I so earnestly advise, I am persuaded, she will be better, and happier, by and by…

I cannot close my letter without again begging you to give my love to your sister, with a repetition of the assurance, that she may count upon my doing all I can for her; and that her having too often prevented my doing the best I could, will never deter me from doing whatever may remain in my power. Tell her to consider what I have urged, and not reject it too

> *hastily. Removal and skilful medical treatment are, in the first instance, absolutely and immediately necessary – half measures never answer, and feeble ones but seldom.*
>
> – 9 August 1833

Soon it was the eve of her departure from Paris, and it was time to say goodbye to Maria Barlow. She called at Mrs Barlow's at twenty-five minutes past ten in the morning on 17 August. Mrs Barlow brought up the subject of their letters exchanged over the years.

> *She asked about burning my letters. Said she might keep or destroy, or do just what she liked with them, quite easy about it. She had thought it right to try to forget. Did not, would not say she had succeeded. Might have had a scene. The tears were in her eyes but I was too calm and philosophic. Jane left us and was coming away without saluting, but Mrs Barlow willed it otherwise and I kissed her kindly but no more and quietly walked off. Will be very civil, kind and attentive but no more nonsense, whether she would or not.*
>
> – 17 August 1833

After several weeks of a cool reception and polite conversation, Anne left Maria Barlow. Poor Mrs Barlow. Her only fault was in loving Anne too much.

With Mrs Barlow now behind her and Paris shrinking on the horizon, Anne turned her attention to her new adventure with Sophie Ferral. '*Mademoiselle Ferral and I get on very well,*' she wrote optimistically in her diary on 18 August. They left Paris mid-afternoon, a little party of Anne, her two servants, Miss Ferral and her little dog. They overnighted at Meaux, pausing their journey after four hours on the road. At Meaux, a '*narrow streeted little town but prettily situated,*' they visited the Cathédrale Saint-Étienne de Meaux, '*very neat and handsome – the white or yellow wash had been carefully scraped off. Monument seated of Boussuet, whose church and see this was*'. Jacques-Bénigne Bossuet was a French bishop with the jurisdiction of the Diocese of Meaux. Today, there are three monuments commemorating Bossuet in the Meaux Cathedral. The oldest one, by Ruxthiel, a Belgian sculptor, which was admired by Anne, was installed in 1822. It details the bishop seated on the papal throne with his right arm raised. The more impressive one which can be seen today, was sculpted by Dubois and inaugurated in 1911. The third monument is Bossuet's funeral slab, laid in 1704 by his nephew, abbot of Saint Lucien de Beauvais and archdeacon of Meaux. In 1854, realising that the original slab had deteriorated beyond repair, the

State replaced it with black marble and reproduced the inscription which appeared on the original.

From Meaux they were soon at La Ferté-sous-Jouarre, where they were detained for forty minutes, *'mending the broken screw of the bride du corps d'Essieu (bed-brace, off fore-wheel)'* and where Anne had observed a *'nice little town celebrated for meules à moulin[7], best in France, and lying all along the river side'*. Anne's observation was accurate. La Ferté is indeed famed for its millstones, quarried in the vicinity out of beds of a siliceous cellular rock known as burr stone, indigenous to the freshwater basin of the Marne valley. These stones were sought after for their high percentage of porosity, which kept wearing away, therefore creating new cutting edges which could be used without having to regularly redress the stone. The hard and less-abrasive nature of the stones also produced a white flour from the wheat they ground. From La Ferté-sous-Jouarre to Épernay, their carriage trundled through *'the Marne and its fine valley. Very pretty descent to the town thro' fine avenue of elms. Picturesque town surrounded by picturesque ranges of hill and commanded by old towerless castle. Populous environs – several large good buildings, cottage mills just out of the town. Some of the mills white and arid looking tho' covered with vine – good wine made here from these white limestone hills'*.

---

7. *meules à moulin* (French): grinding wheels, milling stone-wheels

About eleven hours since leaving Meaux, having travelled the modern equivalent of eighty kilometres (about fifty miles), they arrived at Épernay where they alighted at l'Écu. They set off for Moët's champagne cellars.

> *Half hour in Mr Moët's famous caves each of us candle in hand. Miss Ferral and myself and Eugénie. Inscription in memory of Napoleon le Grand having honoured them with a visit in 1807. Huit cent mille bouteilles[8] i.e. 4 years' stock in the cellars (vaults literally) for sell 200,000 bottles per annum. Half lieue of length of vaulting at the regular depth of 30 pieds[9] below the surface.*
>
> – 19 August 1833

She studied the method the winemaker used to riddle the contents of the bottles.

> *The bottles placed on a low rack (en pente[10]), leaning in an angle of about 25 degrees are so put, to clear them for immediate departure. The other bottles arranged as usual with laths between but fitting into notched lath uprights at the ends – a great support and improvement upon the common plan of having no rest but upon the bottles themselves.*
>
> – 19 August 1833

---

8. *huit cent mille bouteilles* (French): eight hundred thousand bottles

9. *pieds* (French): feet

10. *en pente* (French): sloping, inclined

The wines were sold, between three and six shillings, the upper limit reserved for the most premium. The oldest vintage identified during her visit dated to 1825. Known as Moët et Chandon since 1833 (when Pierre-Gabriel Chandon married into the empire), the company has been making champagne since 1743. The champagne caves measure a total of twenty-eight kilometres, spread over a labyrinthic three levels. Workers still riddle their bottles by hand, a sharp rotation performed in increments of anywhere between a quarter to one-eight of a turn. With the exception of electrical fixtures and a few other health and safety related items, the cellars remain unchanged from when Anne Lister visited.

After their tour, they returned to their inn, l'Écu where Anne recorded, *'while at dinner, came a very civil message from him [Mr Moët], begging my acceptance of a bottle of Sillery, and one of pink champagne. The latter was most excellent, tasted so good we drank the whole bottle, and were admirably unfitted for doing anything but go to bed and sleep'*.

Anne and her little group continued their journey east towards Verdun. They stopped briefly at Châlons where she explored on her own. She considered the Cathédrale Saint-Etienne de Châlons-en-Champagne a *'very fine old Gothic building. Very fine (and neat). Within the windows of the side aisles and transept all of beautiful painted glass. Low handsome chapels along the side aisles – modern west front'*. She also visited the handsome Hôtel de Ville de Châlons, remarking that the *'windings of the river (Marne) and bridges over it very picturesque'*. Then, about nine kilometres from Châlons, they gazed upon the Basilique Notre-Dame de L'Epine.

> *Built in the time of Charles VII and Louis XI – a bush being on fire nine days without burning, the identical little image of the Virgin now on the altar (right) entrance to the chancel. Was taken out of the bush over which this said altar now stands and at which miracles are even now (said the priest) still performed! The last was four years ago – a little girl ætatis[11] ten not having any use of her limbs was brought nine days to the messe[12], and placed on the altar and [on] the ninth day recovered the entire use of her limbs and has kept it ever since. Heard all this with such decent gravity, the priest gave me a small printed account of the church and probably miracles too, believing me, no doubt, a good Catholic.*
>
> *– 20 August 1833*

Anne was impressed with Châlons and its surroundings.

> *Châlons (or Chaalons) is a nice town, and interesting on account of its antiquities as having been the capital*

---

11. *ætatis* (Latin): at the age of
12. *messe* (French): mass

of this part of Gaul. It was about 12 or 14 miles from here that the Romans under Aëtius[13] and the Goths under Theodoric[14] defeated Attila and his Huns in 451. The camp of Attila, as it is still called, is close to the little village of Lascheppe[15], five or 6 miles from Somme-Vesle, and now covered with corn-fields, tho' some of the breastworks[16] are still very visible and easily traced for a considerable distance. The great old Roman road passes just above Somme-Vesle. In fact, the whole of this country is classic.

– letter to Aunt Anne, 15 September 1833

Anne very much wanted to visit Camp d'Attila but the roads were bad and not suited for a carriage. The little excursion would have also incurred an extra cost of six shillings for a small, sturdy gig[17] plus the fee of the postilion[18], and would have added nearly three hours to their journey. Anne decided to skip Camp d'Attila. They made Verdun that evening, arriving at the Trois

---

13. Flavius Aetius (Roman general, lived circa 391-454).
14. Theodoric I (king of the Visigoths between 418 and 451).
15. La Cheppe, 11 kilometres north of Somme-Vesle. Camp d'Attila is about 600 metres from La Cheppe.
16. Temporary military fortification, often of earth, built up to chest height to provide defensive protection.
17. Light, two-wheeled cart mounted with a chair or chaise, pulled by a horse.
18. Person who drives the horse pulling the vehicle.

Maures at five minutes to eight, where Anne, *'very much bargained, and as the woman wanted at last to make me pay four shillings additional for the empty beds in one large, double-bedded room au premier[19] went upstairs into small single bedded rooms, determined to keep to the arrangement of twenty shillings pour tout[20]. Dinner at 8 ¾ plentiful and very good – nothing to complain of but the wine'*. The two ladies parted at ten to their respective rooms. They seemed to be sharing some intimate details, with Anne recording in her diary, *'Miss Ferral has her cousin[21] come or coming today'*. Then funnily enough, the next day, Anne *'found my cousin came'*.

Decades later, the town of Verdun was to play an important but bloody role in World War I.

On 21 February 1916, the Germans launched an attack on Verdun – a veritable deluge of shells. This marked the beginning of the Battle of Verdun during WWI which was to last for three hundred days. Entrenched on a battlefield enclosed by the hills of Verdun, some two million men fought in harsh conditions. For more than ten months, the German and French soldiers fought along a line that never exceeded thirty-five kilometres

---

19. *au premier* (French): on the first floor
20. *pour tout* (French): for everything
21. *cousin*: Anne's term for menstruation

in length. An estimated sixty million shells fell on the Verdun region in 1916.

In March 1916, temperatures fell to minus fifteen degrees Celsius. Soldiers under siege, trapped in their trenches of mud, rain and snow, had no access to the rear and were forced to drink polluted water. Some resorted to their own urine.

Dead bodies littered the ground, disappearing into the quagmire of mud, resurfacing as the ground was pounded by shells. Survivors fighting on the front were faced with their compatriot's dismembered and decomposing bodies around them; on which they had to tread in narrow communications trenches and under which they sought shelter.

On the hills around Verdun, about 163,000 French soldiers and 143,000 German soldiers lost their lives. If these men were lined up next to each other on the ground, they would stretch in an unbroken line over a distance of about 215 kilometres – the distance between Paris and Verdun.

Verdun was not the bloodiest battle of WWI, but it was etched into people's minds by the presence of dead bodies that remained on the battle fields with the living soldiers. The shelling made it nearly impossible to remove the bodies.

In the end, the Battle of Verdun had no effect on the situation along the western front. The battle produced some 700,000 casualties. About 300,000 were killed or considered missing, and a further 400,000 were wounded.

Fifty years later, Charles de Gaulle in a speech said, 'Based on the events that took place during the battle, neither French nor German troops can say that they gained anything but pain from all the fighting'.

Anne's visit to Verdun was more peaceful and uplifting. She explored the small town and bought some *dragées*, almonds coated with a sugar casing. The confectioner *Braquier*, has been producing *dragées* from its factory in Verdun since 1783. The company still has a shop in Verdun's old quarter at 3 Rue Pasteur and conducts guided tours at its *usine*[22] on the outskirts, 50 Rue du Fort de Vaux, where visitors can join a tour and see how *dragées* are made and admire the antique implements.

She also visited the Cathédrale Notre-Dame de Verdun, and gazed upon the many paintings that hung on the pillars along the nave, noting '*none good*' and the four green '*handsome, twisted marble columns of [the] high altar*'. She peeped into the *archevêché*[23] now repurposed as the Centre Mondial de la Paix, and considered it a '*very good house – said to be one of the best palais épiscopaux*[24] *in*

---

22. *usine* (French): factory
23. *archevêché* (French): archbishopric, the jurisdiction or office of an archbishop
24. *palais épiscopaux* (French): episcopal palace, bishop's residence

France'. She walked along the ramparts of the Citadelle Haute, which in 1833 was used as a prison.

> ...*where our prisoners were confined during the war – poorish looking range of building. Saw military prisoners, deserters kept there now. Walked on the ramparts, and the promenade called La Roche from whence they say the view is very fine. Not at all – would be if there was wood, but there is none. The hills are too bare, chiefly vines with patches of corn and tho' our officers on paroles had a range of 2 lieues from the ville[25], they must have found it deadly dull.*
>
> – 21 August 1833

They left Verdun in the afternoon and now headed north-east towards Longwy for the night, the *'hills bare till about half way from Verdun to Étain then clothed with wood and very pretty. Better land, the verdure[26] reminds one of England. Nothing like it about Paris or all the way. Great deal of rape in flower. Étain about 3,000 inhabitants – make cloth and filatures de coton[27] and paper. Situated on the little river Orne'*.

Unknown to Anne, in the cool, dim silence of the unassuming church of St Martin, along the route she would have taken, a stone's throw from the Orne, is

---

25. *ville* (French): city
26. *verdure* (French): greenery
27. *filatures de coton* (French): cotton mills

Ligier Richier's finest sculpture of the lamentation of Virgin Mary, called La Pietà[28]. Richier was born in Saint-Mihiel, about fifty kilometres south of Étain, circa 1500 and spent the majority of his sculpting career in the duchies of Lorraine and Bar. The splendid sculpture is life-sized, and depicts the grieving Virgin Mary kneeling, supporting on her lap the inanimate body of Jesus Christ. The church, mostly destroyed during World War I, was restored immaculately between 1920 and 1953.

Étain's population seems to have hovered around the three thousand mark for nearly two centuries now. In 1831, census records confirmed 3,034 townspeople, and in 2017, 3,580[29].

From Étain, they passed Spincourt, '*a dirty village. The Poste not an inn, a dirty place*' and then Longuyon where they baited[30] the horses. The valley they travelled through was picturesque, with a pretty little stream along it, and Anne observed that the people were, '*all about here seem well off. Well enough dressed. No beggars, moderate quantity of cattle*'.

They arrived at the Croix d'Or in Longwy for a late supper at quarter to ten, the temperature a pleasant seventeen degrees Celsius for a summer's night. The morning in Longwy dawned with rain on the horizon,

---

28. *La Pietà* (Italian): The Pity
29. Institut National de la Statistique et des Études Économiques
30. bait the horse: to feed and water (a horse or other animal), especially during a journey.

and with Anne lamenting her bodily functions, '*Very much cousin. Near half hour on the pot half asleep, but no motion*'. The rain eventually arrived at half past seven in the morning and stopped her from exploring Longwy, which was a shame. Longwy is an ancient town, magnificently fortified with the seventeenth-century citadel designed by Sébastien Le Prestre de Vauban – the same esteemed military engineer who built the Barrage Vauban and citadel in Strasbourg.

They attempted to wait out the rain, but by ten o'clock, decided to head off to Luxembourg.

> *Off (from Longwy) at ten. The rain had prevented my stirring out. Small, strongly fortified town. Fine country about Longwy. At 10 20/.. stop three or [four] minutes at the little douane*[31] *to shew our passports for the last time in France and almost immediately pass the borne*[32] *between France and the Grand Duchy of Luxembourg. Stop at the Luxembourg douane at 10 ¾ – expected to be searched, not even a question asked, just looked at our passports and let us drive off.*
>
> – 22 August 1833

Within three hours of crossing the border, they arrived at Luxembourg city. They entered the first gate

---

31. *douane* (French): customs
32. *borne* (French): border, boundary

and clattered along narrow stone roads, *'just like English roads'* and alighted at the Hôtel de Cologne where they were greeted by the *'good humoured, fat landlady'*. They were not staying the night but passing through, hoping to make headway towards Prussian territory.

In Luxembourg, there was *'nothing to be seen in the town but the citadel, but several curiosities in the neighbourhood'*, according to Anne. The citadel, on the hilltop of Montée de Clausen provides wonderful, expansive views of the Alzette, and the fifteenth-century Stierchen Bridge that spans it, along with the pretty grounds of the St Jean du Grund church. But what is more captivating than the citadel is the eighteenth-century Bock Casemates, a series of honeycomb rock galleries and passages carved out of the rock during the Spanish rule. During the French Revolutionary Wars, the citadel and casemates proved impregnable. When the city eventually surrendered after a seven-month siege by the French, their walls remained unbreached. During World War I and II, the casemates again came to the rescue of its citizens and provided shelter during shelling. To this day, the casemates are open for visitors and worth a visit.

Luxembourg's Cathédrale Notre-Dame, *'a small good old church'*, was considered by Anne to be unique for the *'plaster of the pillars of the nave marked out in a pattern'*. The arabesque detail on the pillars is one of the first things that a modern visitor might notice when entering the church. The cathedral has withstood the many

Paris to Luxembourg

power struggles over the centuries, emerging mostly unscathed. Declaring Luxembourg '*a small but good and very neat, clean town*', Anne and her group left the city.

In driving thro' the gateway, broke the sabot[33] – 25 minutes getting it mended. Fine rich wooded beautiful country all round Luxembourg. Fine road thro' avenue of young poplars but pavé again at 4 25/.. for the rest of the way. At first very bad, then as remarkably good for the rest of the way to Grevenmacher. Everywhere good crops. Great many plots of potatoes. Stop at 5 5/.. for ¼ hour to bait the horses. Several villages scattered picturesquely about – vines again on the hill-side (left) just before entering Grevenmacher at 6 35/.. Would not go farther for fear of darkness and missing the scenery.

– 22 August 1833

Anne had written in her diary, somewhat diplomatically that Grevenmacher was merely a '*tolerable little town,*' but to her aunt, she was more candid, '*nobody but myself would have slept at Grevenmacher*'. But Grevenmacher had its saving grace. The Moselle

---

33. *sabot* (French): drag shoe – piece of wood or metal which is applied to a wheel in a braking system for carts and carriages pulled by horses. It was especially important for steep hills when the weight of the cart could push the horse over. The shoe would be fitted over the back wheel to stop it rotating and cause it to slow. Once at the bottom of the hill it would be removed.

flowed alongside the town, and Anne *'walked down to the river – a good one, and very pretty, about like the Ouse at the end of the New Walk, York'*.

The next morning turned out to be *'very fine'* and they set off for Prussia at nine. Anne had a little trouble at the Prussian customs, in the town of Igel, when the officers found that Eugénie's luggage contained two pairs of new leather shoes she had not declared. Duty on her unworn shoes was levied, *'she had more than their full value of duty to pay'* and Eugénie was three thalers, seventeen silver groschen and six pfennige poorer for it. Converted to English currency at the time, it would have been about three shillings, and considering Anne could pawn her umbrella for a shilling, and purchase a kilogramme of butter for about the same, the levy would have been expensive to Eugénie.

The customs officers detained them for an hour and searched through all their belongings before they were allowed to continue onwards to Trêves. Not one to let the delay deter her enthusiasm for Germany, Anne visited the 23-metre tall, richly decorated Igeler Säule, which depicts reliefs of scenes from the life of the Secundinier cloth merchant family and mythology. *'The tomb of the Secundinii at the village'* of Igel was *'very perfect'*. *'About the middle of the village a little farther on (left) stands a very fairly well-preserved Roman sort of pillar surmounted by the Roman Eagle with its head looking broken off'*.

A couple of hours later, *'on descending the hill, fine view of Trêves, straight before us. Fine looking town, the large cathedral and other churches, hospital and barracks having an important appearance'*.

Trêves, or Trier in German, is described by Murray's nineteenth-century travel guide: *'This very ancient city stands on the right bank of the Moselle, in a valley of exuberant richness, surrounded by low, vine-clad hills; it has 14,000 inhabitants*[34]*'*.

Trier is the oldest city in Germany. It was conquered in 16 BC by the Roman emperor Augustus, who called this key city of the Roman northern territories *Augusta Treverorum*[35]. Because of the numerous Roman ruins in the city, it has become known as the *Rome of the North*. At its peak, the city was twice the size it is now. One of Trier's famous sons was Karl Marx, the political theorist, philosopher and economist.

Trier had its own significance for me.

It was the city from which I chose to start my journey, following in Anne's footsteps in the sweltering July of 2019.

---

34. *A Handbook for Travellers on the Continent*, John Murray. Published 1838
35. *Augusta Treverorum* (Latin): 'City of Augustus among the Treveri' (Celtic tribe which founded Trier in 4 BC)

Anne Lister's route through Germany to Travemünde in 1833

Chapter Four

Trier to Einbeck

William Morris, the British poet, novelist and textile designer, once said, *'The true secret of happiness lies in taking a genuine interest in all the details of daily life'*[1]. And to paraphrase one of the teachings of Buddha, to enjoy good health and attain true happiness, one must first discipline and control one's mind. I was determined not to mope about Ziggy – I recognised he had had a full and wonderful fifteen years of life; and that he had been given an additional bonus of four years when he survived an internal haemorrhage due to a ruptured tumour on his spleen sometime in 2016. I prefer to celebrate life, not dwell upon death.

---

1. Morris, William – *The Aims of Art, Signs of Change*, 1888

I understood the theory of the grieving process, I just wasn't very good at translating it into practice. In fact, throwing myself into researching the route, reading and re-reading passages from books written about Anne Lister was therapeutic. In July 2019, transcripts of Anne's diaries of 1833 were not readily available. I was not even aware that one could download her diary pages. Armed just with the scant details that I could find, I pledged to visit major landmarks built before the twentieth century, ascend all cathedral towers, walk everywhere in twenty-five minutes, and eat sumptuous dinners, letting it all fight it out inside and hope my bowels did not suffer as a result.

Anne had a propensity to travel with thermometers. In the 1800s thermometers were as tall as a four-year-old child, and probably weighed half as much. They were encased in quality-wood, solid things one could use as an accessory to murder. I was not about to walk around with something like that, and made do with the digital thermometer on the dashboard of my car.

While Anne travelled with her unwieldy books – diaries, journals, travel handbooks and other reference items – I had merely my guidebooks on Germany and Denmark, and my Kindle device, weighing just 220 grammes, that contained about 350 titles.

I tossed an empty beer crate into the boot of my car. Voltaire once said:

> *Parfait Anglais, voyageant sans dessein,*
> *Achetant cher de modernes antiques,*
> *Regardant tout avec un air hautain,*
> *Et méprisant les saints et leurs reliques*[2]

Voltaire's poem may be translated as, 'Perfect English, travelling without purpose, buying expensive modern antiques, looking at everything with a haughty air, and despising the saints and their relics'. Obviously, Voltaire had not met a Germanised Australian Lister nerd. I was travelling with a purpose, a determination to discover, and my idea of souvenirs was craft beers from the places I visited. The journey was starting to look promising.

Ziggy's ashes returned home on Friday, 5 July 2019. I allowed myself a little cry, and spent a restless night anxious about my journey. There was nothing else holding me back and on Saturday, I packed my bags and left home after saying goodbye to my husband, Chris, who understood this was a journey I had to do alone.

While travelling through Germany, Anne had *'found the inns, however odd-looking, comfortable enough, except for the evil of scanty bedclothes, scarcely large enough to*

---

2. Voltaire – La Pucelle d'Orléans (1762), Chant VIII

cover a person, is universal, just as bad at the great houses as the small'. She would not have known that nearly two hundred years later, the German hospitality industry would still be clueless and have not progressed in this regard. Having suffered German bedding for quite a few years now, I had taken to travelling with my own pillow. I used to think it an unrefined practice but has since capitulated – the atrocious German pillow offers no neck support whatsoever and is equivalent to sleeping on an insignificant, deflated sack of nothing measuring eighty by eighty centimetres. And whatever size bed you get, you are frequently offered a duvet which is single-sized. Germans may engineer the most amazing cars, window systems and autobahns but the comfort of sleep still proves elusive even after two centuries.

In my determination to immerse myself in a positive and uplifting environment, I removed music that had the potential to make me weep, and therefore culled from my playlist the likes of Lisa Stansfield, Edvin Marton, Havasi and Luz Casal. Instead, I was resolute to bop, while driving, to Fine Young Cannibals, DePhazz, Paris Café Society, Clara Luciani and a few other pop bands any self-respecting individual would be too embarrassed to admit to. But mostly, I played on repeat at high volume the theme song to the television programme, *Gentleman Jack*, performed by an English folk music duo from Yorkshire called O'Hooley &

Tidow. Music had always moved me. Rightly or wrongly, it can make me happy or sad, run faster than I normally can or garden more aggressively with my pruners. And so, equipped with a car accessorised with Harman Kardon speakers, I collected my first speeding ticket within the first hundred kilometres of setting off. That was an impressive accomplishment, considering many German autobahns have no speed limits.

Germany in August 1833 was a collection of thirty-nine sovereign states and was on the cusp of the implementation of the *Zollverein*, a customs union quite similar to the free trade of the modern European Union. Prussia played an instrumental role in uniting the German states after the Napoleonic Wars, when it recognised that the fragmented states created an uncompetitive barrier to trade. It sought to remove the barriers between member states and institute a uniform tariff against non-members. Prior to Prussia's push for the *Zollverein*, a trader or traveller like Anne would have been faced with a formidable number of customs barriers throughout Germany. The Prussian customs law of 1818 and the German Confederation *Zollverein* of 1834 ended the restriction on trade growth, and encouraged more efficient travel. As an example, prior to the *Zollverein*, a traveller from Dresden to Magdeburg, a distance of approximately 220 kilometres, would have been subjected to sixteen customs posts. If

Anne had wanted to travel from Trier in western Prussia to Kaliningrad, then in east Prussian territory, she would have been subjected to at least eighty counts of customs clearance[3].

Despite the progressive economic stance of the German Confederation, travel in 1833 was still unlike what we in modern times take for granted. The euro was still more than 150 years away and Anne would have had to manage complicated foreign currency calculations. The denomination of British money in 1833 was complicated enough, but coupled with the Prussian denominations, made for complex calculations worthy of Archimedes.

At Grevenmacher, Anne bought sixty thalers at an exchange of 3.75 for 225 francs; and in a diary entry a week prior, gave a clue on the exchange rate between the French and English currencies when she wrote, '... *she allows her maid 2s/6d English or 3 francs French a week for washing*'. Twelve pennies made one shilling, which meant three francs divided by 2 1/2 shillings would equal one franc and twenty centimes. In Prussia, thirty silver groschen or twenty-four gute groschen made one thaler; and twelve pfennige equalled one silver groschen. This meant that one thaler, equal to 3.75 francs was therefore

---

3. Seidel, Friedrich – *Das Armutsproblem im deutschen Vormärz bei Friedrich List. Kölner Vorträge zur Sozial und Wirtschaftsgeschichte*, volume 13, Köln 1971, s. 4

the equivalent of approximately three English shillings. Thankfully, the currency of Prussia was accepted throughout the whole of northern Germany and even in Frankfurt and Nassau, where florins and kreutzers were more predominant. In Hessian, Hanoverian and Brunswick territories, the denominations were also in thaler and silver groschen. One gold coin, be it the Frederick, Wilhelm or Georgen d'or, was equal to five thalers and twenty silver groschen. To decomplicate the exchange rate, the Prussian, Hessian, Hanoverian and Brunswick territories equalised the value of the thaler among the states. However, to further confound the traveller, the values marked on German coins were very often not truly the coin's face value. The double Hessian Frederick d'or, worth eleven thalers and ten silver groschen was stamped with X (ten) Thaler, and in the south, the silver pieces marked ten and twenty kreutzers were worth twelve and twenty-four[4]. Even Anne blamed the German currency for preventing her from writing earlier to her aunt.

> *I meant to have written to you from somewhere or other long since; but could not make up my mind to send you a short, good-for-nothing letter, and have never had time to write comfortably – for, after sight-seeing, and keeping a tolerably regular account of*

---

[4]. Murray, John – *A Handbook for Travellers on the Continent*, 2nd edition, section IV, published 1838

> *German money (the most tiresome in the world?) one is generally glad enough to go to bed.*
>
> – 15 September 1833

Anne and her small entourage crossed '*a handsome stone bridge over the river and alight at the Maison Rouge in the Grand Place, Trêves*' just a little after noon. The Maison Rouge[5] still stands in the main square of Trier. It was built in 1684 in late Renaissance style and located on the west side of Hauptmarkt. Along the front facade above the windows to the second floor is the inscription '*Ante Roman Treviris stetit annis mille trecentis; prestet et æterna pace frvatvr. Amen*', which translates into 'Trier stood 1,300 years before Rome; may it ever thrive and enjoy eternal peace'.

She immediately set about bargaining for a room. The proprietor '*wanted 24 francs a day. An English lady and gentleman and child and femme du chambre pay 22 franc. Stood out for all at 5 thalers a day and got it*'. Anne had bargained just about three francs off list price. Pleased with herself, she and Miss Ferral set off for the sights of Trier.

> *To the Roman Gateway, then to the Roman Baths, lately cleaned out and still in progress of further*

---

5. Rotes Haus, Fleischstraße 3, 54290 Trier

cleaning at the expense of the King (of Prussia). 4000 troops here and 8000 ditto at Luxembourg. The baths a fine venue. The man from there went with us to the gateway (of which he has the care) and shewed us up to what was the top church. Two churches in the two storeys below – easily converting into these churches by adding one old circular Saxon building at one end for the sacristies and high altars.

The French when here wantonly pulled down the top storey of one of the two Roman Towers of the gateway. They were let loose upon the unhappy town and getting to all the store of wine in the cellars of the thirty convents; were besides themselves – quite voleurs[6] – took everything they fancied from everybody they met. Then strolled by ourselves to the church of St Paulin, celebrated for its painted plafonds. Very striking and handsome – not large but very handsome church. Thence to the amphitheatre which the king is cleaning out. The arena and some of the vomitoria[7] just laid open but no benches as yet.

– 23 August 1833

---

6. *voleurs* (French): thieves

7. Passage below a Roman amphitheatre from which performers or gladiators enter or exit the arena, and may also be used to provide rapid egress for large crowds of spectators.

Together with Miss Ferral, Anne explored the town, and recorded the price of meat, '*7 pennies a pound*', the price of renting a horse, '*half a thaler or one thaler a day*', and the cost of a good horse, '*fifteen to twenty écus[8] (thalers)*'. She looked in vain for a guidebook of Trier.

Now on day six of their travels together, Anne and Miss Ferral were on good terms.

> *Miss Ferral and I get on very well. It is quite evident she likes me. Joked her this evening about helping me to furnish a house here. She would do it for me; would come to me anywhere, in any hole.*
>
> – 23 August 1833

The next morning, before leaving for Wittlich, Anne walked down to the Römerbrücke, the same bridge over the Moselle that her carriage had crossed over, built by the Romans during the time of Antoninus Pius. She wrote that she, '*walked down to the fine eight-arched bridge over the Moselle (as wide here as the Thames at Richmond) that we crossed on entering the town yesterday*'. There was only one old bridge which spanned the Moselle near the customs house she described at that time. The Römerbrücke is likely the oldest monument in Trier and

---

8. The *écu* was a French gold coin. Though it was replaced by the 5-franc silver coin in the nineteenth century, the French people continued to call the piece *écu*. Anne however, referred to the thaler sometimes in the French term *écu* – very likely for the Prussian *écu* (coat of arms) on the coin.

mentioned by Roman historian, Tacitus, who lived in the first and second centuries. At the height of Trier's might, the bridge demarcated the middle of the town, but now, the old town is contained to a small section about one and a half kilometres away. The only ancient parts remaining are the piers of large stones built from black basalt from the dormant volcanic mountain range of the Eifel about 120 kilometres north east.

Like Anne, I too explored Trier, but with a zest and purpose superior to the average ambling tourist. I scrambled upon the ruins of the Roman Amphitheatre and explored the cool dungeons underneath. I sweltered in temperatures exceeding thirty degrees Celsius as I walked among the ruins of the Kaiserthermen baths and marvelled at the Porta Nigra – a tremendous, ancient Roman city gate dating back to the second century held together miraculously by nothing but gravity and iron clamps. In the dim lighting of the Liebfrauenkirche, I gazed upon the tomb of St Theodulphus, said to be son of a British prince, who eschewed his princely life and exiled to Gaul in 500 AD and joined the priesthood, *'his statue recumbent above and his real body, minus half the foot and the head, below'*, and explored the same cloisters that Anne walked through when she visited the Dom Trier.

The unassuming Basilica of St Paulinus, 1,200 metres from the Dom Trier on the outskirts of the old town of Trier is easy to miss. I did not know of its existence on my first trip to Trier, but returned after I learnt of it when transcribing Anne's diary. St Paulinus's exterior is modest and does not command a grand appearance. Many tourists do not walk the distance to visit this church, and it is considered unworthy of modern guidebooks. When I found the convent of St Maximin that Anne had said was converted into barracks, I was disappointed. The building was nondescript and fenced up, and around the grand stone portal was piled construction material and rubbish. I did not have much expectation for St Paulinus, but I continued my walk along Thebäerstraße. I have to admit, at first glance, St Paulinus was not particularly impressive and the heavy wooden doors were shut. Pessimistically I thought them most likely locked, but I pushed against them and they opened.

The sight that greeted me rendered me speechless. The beautiful and unsurpassable Baroque plafonds[9] with its intricate detail painted high above the nave which Anne admired and wrote about, is spectacular and captivating. Never before had I seen something like this. Painted in 1743 by Christoph Scheffler, the plafonds depict the story of St Paulinus, who is buried in the basilica's crypt, and the martyrdom of the Theban Legion, a Roman garrison which was massacred

---

9. plafond: an ornately decorated or painted ceiling

en masse for its unwavering Christian faith. A talent capable of creating such a divine marvel like this must have been blessed by the Gods themselves. I stood there, in silence for a long time, in awe and quietly thanked Anne Lister for bringing me back to Trier.

Just before they left Trier, Anne settled the bill for their rooms and board at the Maison Rouge. Her delight at initially getting a reduction of three francs was obliterated when presented with a bill of seven. '*The servants had dined and the man charged wine extra, so that the agreement for 5 thalers was nugatory and had to pay 7*'. She did not let it dampen her enthusiasm for their journey, especially when at Wittlich, noting that '*Miss Ferral and I in the same room, first time – very fine day*'.

However, by the morning the novelty had worn off.

> ...*not very comfortable. I had no motion. Obliged to go to the little smelling place in the house after being dressed. Miss Ferral sleeps without nightcap and in her day shift. She told me this morning in the carriage, of the Russian Madame de Bourke wished her to marry, an exile. First said he had sixty then forty thousand francs a year. A club foot and twenty-seven years older than herself.*
>
> – 25 August 1833

At the inn in Wittlich, determined to claw back her loss at Maison Rouge, she negotiated hard and this time knew to include wine into the bargain. Four thalers, '*supper, breakfast, beds for us all including wine*'.

They made their onward journey to Koblenz via Lützerath, Kaisersesch and Polch.

> *Beautiful morning and country. No peep of the river – 3 or 4 miles from it. Very hilly stages but good road otherwise (good road ever since entering the Prussian states). The hills beautifully wooded – beech and oak. Heaps of scoriae*[10] *along the road to repair it with. Very fine drive to Lützerath, a mere village but good-looking hotel at the Poste. At least, better looking there than that of last night (cleaner) and where all might have slept very well?*
>
> – 25 August 1833

Before the town of Kaisersesch, Anne encountered what she thought was the Metternich mountain. They required four horses to ascend the steep route and harnessed an additional horse at the village of Lützerath. Exploration of the area between Lützerath and Kaisersesch suggests that, based on her description, she had mistaken the Müllenbach for Metternich, admiring a '*very beautiful gorge. A little in the Pyrenees style – the*

---

10. fragments of basalt rock

autumnal tints beautiful. At the top of the hill, wildish brae[11] *ground with one conical not high summit and one neat cottage not far from the foot'*. The Müllenbach valley, located along her route towards Koblenz, extends south east along the brook valley of the Kaulenbach, and both valleys have been nature reserves since 1988. Hiking trails abound in this area, a beautiful landscape with frequently changing altitudes, and populated with century-old softwood. The gorge, predominantly of slate and greywacke, is cut deep and jagged and the Endertbach snakes through this enchanting valley. Wanting to explore, Anne *'walked down the finely wooded beautiful gorge with little stream at the bottom, and then in 25 minutes up to the top of the Matternach mountain'*.

They arrived at Koblenz just after four in the afternoon of 26 August and after shopping around for accommodation, Anne settled on the Hôtel de Cologne, a *'newly fitted up, very neat and clean'* establishment.

The next morning, while Miss Ferral went to visit her cousin, Mrs Humfrey, Anne went to the bank of Mr Henry Kehrmann, noting that the gentleman was *'very civil – changed £25 circular note 2093 into écus de Prusse at de Brabant-Exchange 6 thalers 73 cents per*

---

11. a steep bank or hillside

pound sterling = 166 thalers 20 silber[12] *groschen of which 62 écus de Brabant and 104 thalers 20 silber groschen'.*
Money matters settled, she explored Koblenz.

> *Then down to the river. Then to the top of the cathedral, up 54 steps and 5 or 6 ladders for the view. The Moselle distinguishable for some distance by the redness of its waters, falls into the Rhine (whiter) opposite Ehrenbreitstein. Interior of cathedral very neat – pillars and all below painted white, the rest whitewashed. Nave arcaded with sort of plain Corinthian capitals to the columns. Roof groined. The four pictures in the chœur*[13] *by Zick*[14] *of Ehrenbreitstein very fair, but the best picture a copy by Van Dyck (reduced I should think one half) of the famous Descent from the Cross at Antwerp by Rubens. Tomb of the Emperor Conrad (who built the church). Opposite the west end is the fountain surmounted by sort of obelisk on which written 'An 1812 mémorable par la campagne contre les Russes sous le Préfecture de Jules Doazan. Vu et approuvé par nous Commandant Russe de la Ville du Coblentz le 1er Janvier 1814'.*
>
> – 26 August 1833

---

12. *silber* (German): silver
13. *chœur* (French): choir
14. Konrad Zick, German portrait and landscape painter (1773-1836).

The first line of the inscription on the Castor fountain reads, 'The year 1812 memorable by the campaign against the Russians under the Prefect Jules Doazan'. Koblenz was once the capital of the Department of the Rhine and Moselle, an administrative unit which was formed during the French Revolutionary Wars. Jules Doazan, the prefect of Koblenz, deeply devoted to Napoleon had prematurely erected a monument celebrating the campaign against the Russians during the Sixth Coalition War in 1812. However, in 1814 when the Russian army corps advanced towards Koblenz, the French promptly evacuated the city. The Russian commander found the inscription on the monument amusing and, in good humour, instructed a stone mason to inscribe a second line placed under the first, which read, 'Seen and approved by us, Russian Commander of the City of Coblentz on 1st January 1814'.

Koblenz was not new to Anne. She had visited in 1829 when she travelled along the Rhine with Lady Caroline Duff Gordon. Lady Gordon was unable to explore Koblenz with Anne due to '*a twist in her bowels*[15]' and so Anne visited the mighty Ehrenbreitstein Fortress with her teenage son, Cosmo Gordon. The fortress, situated 118 metres above the Rhine, is now accessible by a cable car on the west bank of the river near the Basilica of

---

15. 18 September 1829 – WYAS SH:7/ML/E/12/0086

Saint Castor. The fortress provides excellent views of Koblenz and the confluence of the Moselle and Rhine. Napoleonic troops destroyed the fortress in 1801 and it was reconstructed under the orders of the Prussian king, Friedrich Wilhelm III in 1817. On its completion in 1828, a year before Anne first arrived into Koblenz, the fortress was considered one of the mightiest in Europe.

Eager to gain more ground towards Kassel, they left Koblenz that day and travelled on *'capital English-like road'* surrounded by *'beautifully wooded hill and dale, oak, beech and birch, chiefly beech then fine corn land. Good wheat and oats'*. Anne also recorded her observations of the people, *'at Trêves and afterwards (in valley of the Moselle) the caps of the peasant women like casquettes*[16] *– yesterday (lastly) and today women or rather chiefly girls with their hair plaited from before and secured behind with a large silver pin like a blunt, long knife-blade'*. They passed Montabaur, a *'nice little town (goodish church) commanded by inhabited, house-like castle or schloss – gable-ended windows and picturesque old town'*. The baroque castle of Montabaur is prominently situated at the peak of a hill in the Westerwald and visible from the autobahn when driving on the A3 from my home in Bonn to Frankfurt. I had passed this splendid castle many times and the knowledge that she too enjoyed this same view from her

---

16. *casquette* (French): French hat or bonnet with a little visor

carriage made it extra special. The castle has since been repurposed as a hotel and conference centre.

Just after Montabaur she paid the postmaster '*in florins and kreutzer*' for passage through the next stage of road and barriers as they left Prussia behind and entered the territory of Nassau. Anne recorded that she, '*wrote my name in the registration book for strangers at the Poste*'.

The measure of a stage of journey was termed a post, or *poste*, as Anne was wont to say. She was *très Français* and regularly wrote in French despite sometimes complaining she was not '*French enough*'. Each *poste* was two German miles (a German mile measured 7.5 kilometres[17] or 4.66 English miles). Invariably, at the start or end of a *poste*, is an inn very often called *Zur Post* where travellers could sleep and dine in, and fresh horses obtained. These establishments in Prussia were well managed by the government and the postmasters were often a very respectable class of men, frequently retired officers. At every stage, the postmaster presented a printed ticket, which included the charge for horses according to the number required, wheel greasing, ostler[18] and tolls, which must be paid in advance before setting out. Every horse for Anne's carriage would have cost her 12.5 silver groschen per German mile in the provinces

---

17. Močnik, Franc – *Lehrbuch des gesammten Rechnens für die vierte Classe der Hauptschulen in den k.k. Staaten*, published 1846
18. A man employed to look after the horses of people staying at an inn.

bordering on the Rhine river and in Westphalia, and ten silver groschen in other parts of Prussia.

The man driving Anne's carriage was a postilion and he was paid according to the number of horses he drove – generally ten to twelve silver groschen per German mile when driving up to three horses and eighteen to twenty silver groschen when driving four horses. A postilion was allowed to drive up to a maximum of five horses and was paid in proportion to the number. On average, the German mile took three-quarters of an hour by carriage when driven with three horses under Anne's direction, but generally averaged an hour when driven according to the pace comfortable with the postilion. German postilions were well known for their slowness and diligence on the road, a fact Anne experienced and bemoaned to her aunt in a letter, '*I thought the French driving slower than ever; but it was rapid compared with the German, so that one is off early and arriving late for what one of our mail coaches would do in 5 or 6 hours*'.

In Prussia, though turnpikes[19] occurred at intervals of half a German mile, all charges for roads and barriers would have been included in the postmaster's ticket and were paid to him – a great convenience for travellers.[20]

---

19. Toll barrier or gate
20. Murray, John – *A Handbook for Travellers on the Continent*, 2nd edition, section IV, published 1838

Several *meilen*[21] after Montabaur, Anne encountered the Lahn, a tributary of the Rhine, which she critiqued as *'not so good at the moment as the Calder at Salterhebble'*, and where their carriage trundled over the old stone bridge into Limburg. Limburg is a very ancient town on the Lahn and its Romanesque-Gothic cathedral, Dom zu Limburg high above the town, is said to have been founded in 910 AD. Anne and Miss Ferral *'went to the cathedral; very old. Richly carved pulpit. Church a little in the style of Beverly Minster. Went to the top for the view – two other churches in the little town. Very old, very narrow streets – about 3,000 inhabitants'*.

Limburg today is a delight to wander in, the narrow-cobbled streets flanked by old taverns and beer houses, and quaintly lopsided timber-framed buildings. One of them, the *Haus der Sieben Laster* (House of the Seven Sins), is a heritage-listed sixteenth-century building with a facade adorned with carvings of the seven biblical vices of lust, gluttony, greed, sloth, wrath, envy and pride.

The next morning, it was time to gain more ground, and she set her sights on getting to Marburg, about ninety kilometres away. They set off at ten minutes past seven with four horses, in anticipation of the hilly terrain. Their travels rewarded them with fine views of

---

21. *meilen* (German): miles

'large elms and forest or orchards... well-wooded country... picturesque ruins' as they journeyed through towns such as Weilburg, Braunfels, Wetzlar and Gießen toward Marburg.

Weilburg, *'the handsome, very beautifully situated town'* with its *'large old neglected palace of the Dukes of Nassau'* is now a glorious town. It sits cradled by the Lahn, the river running in a horse shoe-like design round it. The old neglected palace Anne mentioned in 1833 has since been restored to its former glory. The palace is placed on a high vantage point, with its impressive *orangerie*[22] and gardens. Anne thought she *'could live here very well, if could have books and some society'*.

They continued onwards.

> *At 11 ¾ barrier between Nassau and Prussia and enter the latter thro' avenue of Lombardy poplars – charming country all along.*

> *Braunfels (now Prussian) with its château on the top of conical hill imposing and picturesque. Wind up the steep approach. Stop a minute or 2 at the doaune, but they let us off without searching at 12 ¼.*

> *Wetzlar at 1 21/.. a nice-looking old town on the Lahn – 4000 inhabitants. Wind up the steep town thro' very narrow curious old streets. Fine old*

---

22. *orangerie* (French): orangery – a greenhouse or conservatory dedicated to house orange and other fruit trees during winter

church almost at the top of the town, the greater part unglazed and in ruins. The town stands like Weilburg amid orchards and gardens. Not far (from Wetzlar) an isolated conical hill, picturesque ruins of old castle and on another hill (opposite) at some distance, one tall thin round tower. Several of the round topt isolated hills in the country are crowned with churches and towns or ruined castles.

– 27 August 1833

When I visited Braunfels, it appeared as though straight out of a fairy tale. The weather was perfect. The blue skies vibrant, the air invigorating. After exploring the castle, I sat in the little market place with my hazelnut gelato and admired the view.

The castle of Braunfels was the strong-hold of the Counts of Solm in the thirteenth century. It still belongs to the Counts of Solms-Braunfels today. The castle was originally a defence post against the Counts of Nassau and was expanded and remodelled over the centuries. When Anne Lister passed through in 1833, it was used as a governing seat of the princely Solms-Braunfels government. The approach to the castle is steep indeed. The castle itself is situated prominently on the summit of a basalt hill and visible as one approaches in either the direction of Wetzlar or Weilburg.

Wetzlar's four thousand inhabitants in 1833 has now swelled to about 300,000, its economy powered by engineering and steel processing industries. The approach into Wetzlar is disappointingly unromantic and urban, but once in the old town, Wetzlar's true beauty reveals itself. The buildings date back to the 1700s, some, mid-1600s. They are wonderfully restored and preserved, and it is a delight to stroll along the cobbled streets that meander through the town.

The Wetzlar Cathedral had its foundations established around 800 AD and was improved and rebuilt over the centuries. Within the town itself, the cathedral is hidden from view and one follows signs for the Dom[23] through a meandering maze lined with ancient architecture, ascending higher into the heart of Wetzlar. I rounded a corner and was almost rudely dropped into the spacious cathedral square, Domplatz, the cathedral looming over me. If the founding fathers of Wetzlar had deliberately chosen to design the town and cathedral this way to surprise and amaze the average visitor, they have not failed.

The picturesque ruins that Anne saw was of the old imperial castle of Kalsmunt. The castle was named Carols Mons after Charlemagne who ordered its construction around 785 AD and it was an imperial mint around the

---

23. *Dom* (German): cathedral

twelfth century. But by the sixteenth century, it was no longer of military importance. A pleasant, shaded trail, just beyond the historical stone gate Stadttor zur Burg Kalsmunt, leads from the outskirts of the old town through the woods to the ruins of Kalsmunt.

The other tower that Anne saw from her carriage might very well have been the Säuturm. It is a distance from the Kalsmunt, on another hill, opposite the ruins, and very well preserved and maintained. It was called the Tower of Sows because in 1745, a gate was erected next to the tower to allow passage of pigs kept on the fields just outside the town wall.

Just on the fringe of the old town is an ancient stone bridge. The thirteenth-century, 104-metre long Alte Lahnbrücke is one of the oldest surviving bridges in the Hesse region. This may have been the same bridge over which Anne's carriage crossed the Lahn river as she and her companions entered Limburg.

Twelve hours after leaving Limburg that morning, the weary travellers arrived at the Hessian town of Marburg. Unfortunately, Anne did not form a good impression of Marburg. She was dissatisfied with the *'dirty and disagreeable'* inn and her ordeal was further exacerbated by a *'very bad dinner'*.

For me, Marburg was kinder. The weather was pleasant and warm and my very comfortable, clean hotel, at the foot of the hill was convenient for exploring the old town. Marburg is built on the foot and slopes of this hill and on its peak is the very imposing Landgrafen castle. I strolled to the old market square, overlooked by the impressive old Rathaus, the sixteenth-century town hall. A string quartet was playing Pachelbel's Canon in D by the fountain in the square. It could not have been more idyllic. Marburg was a delightful ancient medieval town; with steep, clean, cobbled streets winding up and up, towards the Landgrafen, lined by beautifully restored and preserved timber-framed homes.

Halfway along the steep ascent to the castle is the Philipps University, the world's oldest learning institution, established in 1527. The Brothers Grimm studied law here in the early 1800s and they used their time in Marburg well, gathering old folk tales which they later adapted into their famous stories. The people of Marburg honour the brothers with a walking trail – the Grimm fairy tale path – which runs from Steinweg to the Landgrafen castle along which sculptures depicting their fairy tales are placed.

That evening, I enjoyed a cold beer at an outdoor table overlooking the old square and Rathaus and later dined in the Ratsschänke on a delicious and generous meal. I was truly taken with Marburg and promised to return once more.

The next morning, I rose early. Before crowds gathered in the heat of the day, I was eager to get to Kassel to walk the grounds of the Wilhelmshöhe Bergpark and ascend the Hercules monument, the 71-metre-tall monument crowned with an 8.3-metre-tall copper statue built between 1701 and 1717 that Anne wrote about in her diary.

> *Fine drive. At the Hercules in an hour. The wood about the palace not old, almost all spruce fir – higher up the hill fine old beech forest. The grounds and winding drive up the hill the most à l'Anglais and finest I have yet seen abroad. The Palace D'Hercule château d'eau or whatever they call it, is the large rough building surmounted by a gigantic bronze statue, that one sees from all directions approaching Cassel. The famous water works commence (the fall) from the feet of the building, but all has been long out of order and the great building itself is propped from behind. The present Elector[24] will do nothing, nor will the town of Cassel and the people are dissatisfied to pay 300,000 thalers of revenue to a prince who leaves his wife (sister to the King of Prussia) to live with his favourite comtesse[25] and spend his money anywhere but at home.*
>
> *– 29 August 1833*

---

24. A Prince-Elector or Elector was one of the highest-ranking princes of the German Holy Roman Empire. As an Electoral College, the Electors had the sole right to elect the Roman-German Emperor since the 13th century. While the roles of Electors were abolished in 1806, the ruler of Hesse-Kassel continued to use the title until 1847.

25. In 1821, the Elector of Hesse, Wilhelm II elevated his mistress, Emilie Ortlöpp, to the rank of countess. She was ennobled Countess of Reichenbach-Lessonitz. She bore him eight children. Wilhelm II and Countess Reichenbach-Lessonitz were finally able to marry upon the death of his wife, Princess Augusta of Prussia, in 1841.

Thinking back, I do not know why I was so worried about crowds and heat because it was cloudy and 9.5 degrees Celsius when I got there, with no tourists. At Teufelsbrücke[26], halfway between the palace of Wilhelmshöhe and the Hercules, the scale and height of the monument suddenly seemed rather daunting. My guidebook had failed to mention that it was a 539-step[27] hike just from the grotto of Neptune, at the base of the monument. I berated myself for pledging to walk anywhere in twenty-five minutes and for not having had anything to eat that morning. In any case, I set off at a steady pace and by the time I was nearing the higher levels, I was perspiring in the most unlady-like fashion. I was in a t-shirt and shorts. How Anne managed the same climb in petticoats and stays is a feat in itself. I got to the top in eighteen minutes, my Fitbit declaring I had just climbed an equivalent to a total of sixty-six flights of stairs from the Teufelsbrücke.

At the Hercules monument, Anne climbed into the structure and admired the expansive views over Kassel.

> *Went up last by 3 or 4 ladders into the very body of the Hercule. Magnificent prospect from the platform of the building round the foot of the steeple, on the top of which is placed the Hercule. Fine view over Cassel*

---

26. *Teufelsbrücke* (German): Devil's bridge
27. 539 steps if one ascends on the right and 535 if on the left.

– the palace almost, as it were, at our feet. And at a little distance right embosomed in beech woods, the old castle of Löwenburg (Lionbourg).

All charming but sadly, tired of waiting for the insignificant cascades below at 4 25/.. Had they been constant, the scenery would have been very pretty but the thought that so many people were waiting for a mere exhibition of a few minutes twice a week (Sundays and Thursdays) made the whole too childish. The fountain however, for the ten minutes it played, was very pretty.

– 29 August 1833

The waterworks mentioned by Anne cascade from a large basin at the base of a stone pyramid on which stands the Hercules, then down a stone structure flanked on both sides by stone steps. It flows into the Neptune basin below, interrupted by three oval pools at various levels. The height difference, from Hercules's head to the bottom of the cascade is 179 metres. Just as in 1833, the cascade does not flow constantly and only takes place every Wednesday, Sunday and public holiday between 1 May and 3 October at two thirty in the afternoon.

In Kassel, the cold that Anne contracted in Marburg worsened, and her limbs ached. She found her inn uncomfortable, the bed damp, the tea bad and declared her street *'the essence of dullness'*. But even all this did not stop her from exploring Kassel, and she toured the ten rooms of the museum at the Friedrichsplatz, where she viewed '*several pieces of English clockwork from London – but nothing particular worth notice. But the old coins and medals well-arranged under glass on the tables and the models of the most celebrated ruins at Rome – these done in cork by an Italian artist, and very good*'. She visited an art gallery where she admired some fine pieces from Rubens, Rembrandt, van Dyck and Titian. She thought it '*a valuable collection, but sadly ill lighted (sadly too much glare)*'. She continued her whirlwind tour of Kassel despite her illness.

> *Then to the bain de marbre – really very handsome. A large handsome bath under a marble canopy in a magnificent marble hall, full of good sculpture. The orangery here, something wants paint or repairs of some sort. The oranges larger than those in Paris and full of fruit. Looked over the Kattenbourg, the shell of a castle built up to about the floor of the premier by the last Elector and thus left – looking like the wall round some intended prison-court. The palace de la Residence a handsome looking Ionic portico otherwise plain red sandstone building.*
>
> – 30 August 1833

The fact that I, nearly two hundred years later, could find and see the things she saw and recorded in her diary, never failed to delight me. The *bain de marbre*[28] still stands in the state park near the orangery she mentioned, the orangery itself now repurposed into a planetarium[29]. The ruins of the Chattenburg unfortunately, has been demolished as a result of damage from an air raid on Kassel during World War II.

From Kassel, I followed her trail to Göttingen, the university town of Lower Saxony, nestled near the border of Hesse. Göttingen, in the earlier part of the 1800s, was remarkable only for its university. Murray's Handbook described it as a town *'destitute of fine buildings, and the houses, though old, are neither venerable nor picturesque in their antiquity*[30]*'*. Göttingen had its charm but under no circumstance was it comparable to Trier, Limburg or Marburg. Visitors today can explore the university campus, just outside of the old town and stroll in its botanic garden accessible via a narrow, dark atmospheric tunnel, which is part of its old ancient fortification.

Anne was well prepared for Göttingen. In Paris she had requested letters of introduction to the faculty and Alexandre Brongniart, Anne's former lecturer in mineralogy at the *Jardin des Plantes*, had supplied

---

28. Marmorbad, an der Karlsaue 20D, Kassel
29. Planetarium und Astronomisch-Physikalisches Kabinett, an der Karlsaue 20C, Kassel
30. Murray, John – *A Handbook for Travellers on the Continent*, 2nd edition, section V, published 1838

her with the required documents. First, she called on Johann Friedrich Ludwig Hausmann, a renowned mineralogist, geologist and soil scientist. Hausmann had an impressive resume and would have been a busy man, but the letter Brongniart wrote for Anne must have made a good impression. When Hausmann learnt Anne was standing downstairs, he *'sent down to beg to see me'* and so Anne *'walked up and sat ¾ hour with him – a tall, well countenanced, agreeable, civil man'*. Anne asked him about going to the Brocken, the highest point of the Harz which peaks at 1,141 metres. Hausmann advised Anne that *'the time very good'* for the Brocken, but was *'afraid of the weather'*.

In addition to Hausmann, Anne also had the opportunity to meet the esteemed Johann Friedrich Blumenbach, the *'professor celebrated of comparative anatomy'*.

> *Mr Blumenbach is above 80 (84) but received me with as much vivacity and pleasure and civil as if he had been 30 or 40 years younger but it was easy to see nature could not support this exertion for very long. His countenance still fine, with an agreeable expression of goodness – his voice thick, I with difficulty understood his French. Said I was English and found he spoke English much more intelligently than French, and apparently with much more ease. He promised to shew me his cabinet if I would call*

again at 4 p.m. tomorrow. I complimented him on his looking so well. He said he minded not long life, but to be useful, that was another thing. His wife older than himself and much more infirm but he stoops a good deal, has a little rheumatism and is evidently un vieillard[31].

– 31 August 1833

I was very impressed that Anne had met Blumenbach. He was at the forefront of the scientific community in Germany and is today considered an essential founder of zoology and anthropology, both now recognised as scientific disciplines[32]. He was also one of the founders of scientific anti-racism. Blumenbach argued that there are five distinct races of mankind within a single species, a conclusion he derived from detailed studies of skulls and human anatomy. Although Blumenbach recognised distinct races, he also believed in the unity of the human species, and he combated the use of anthropology as a means to promote discrimination[33]. He had a career which spanned nearly sixty years and gave lectures on

---

31. *un vieillard* (French): an old man
32. I. Jahn, R. Löther, K. Senglaub: *Geschichte der Biologie, Theorien, Methoden, Institutionen, Kurzbiographien.* Jena 1985, s. 637
33. MacCord, Kate, *Johann Friedrich Blumenbach (1752-1840).* Embryo Project Encyclopaedia (2014-01-22). ISSN: 1940-5030 http://embryo.asu.edu/handle/10776/7512

natural history, comparative anatomy, physiology and the history of medicine.

Anne returned with Miss Ferral to visit Blumenbach the next day; after she had *'incurred a cross just before getting up, thinking of Miss Walker'* and had a *'good motion, perhaps that will do me good'*. Blumenbach was delighted to see her and showed them his cabinet of skulls.

> *Blumenbach shewed us into his cabinet of skulls. Observed that same sort of model as the one at the museum – the original, he said, is at Darmstadt (Hesse Darmstadt). It was picked up in some churchyard and bought by the duke at a great price. Mr Jussieu of Paris has one, and there is a third at Prague. The complaint had no name till Blumenbach himself gave it that of osteonecrosis.*
>
> *He has a specimen of a dried man taken from a church in Magdeburg[34] much finer specimen than the one at the museum – no accounting for this kind of drying. Cannot tell why it should be, especially why one should be so dried among so many which perish like the rest.*

---

34. Nedlitz mummies: there were seven mummified corpses, but those said to be of Johanna Juliane Pforte (later found to be the remains of a younger man) and Robert Christian von Hake who died more than 250 years ago, were in the best condition. The mummies were found in the crypt of the village church of Nedlitz, near Magdeburg in Saxony Anhalt.

> *Blumenbach never could make out the great distinguishing mark of a Jew till breakfasting one morning with Sir Benjamin West. He (West) told him it was the ridge formed by the suture of the 2 bones, just under the nose, into which the upper teeth are set. On returning home he found this remark verified and pointed out to me a Jew's skull that was a remarkable illustration of the observation.*
>
> *Spoke of the cave of Bayreuth[35] and of the fossil mammoth[36] on the banks of the Lena.*
>
> – 1 September 1833

Two years after he met Anne, he retired and later passed away at eighty-seven years of age in January 1840. By this time, Blumenbach's skull collection had grown to 245 skulls which he had detailed with accounts of their origin.

Anne also returned to visit Hausmann who took her to the botanical garden and pointed out some trees planted by Albrecht von Haller, a scholar and Swiss botanist who had lectured at Göttingen for a short while. They made

---

35. Teufelshöhle (Devil's Cave) Pottenstein: a dripstone cave in the district of Bayreuth in Bavaria, Germany.
36. The Adams Mammoth, named after Russian botanist Mikhail Adams who journeyed to Siberia to collect its remains. The mammoth was discovered in 1799 in north eastern Siberia near the Lena Delta. Blumenbach, an active naturalist throughout his life, was among the first to describe the woolly mammoth.

plans to meet again the next day, but Anne's strain of cold must have been particularly virulent because Hausmann sent her a note the following morning to let her know he had taken ill. So instead, she visited the library and the museum. *'To the library – above 300,000 volumes – arrangement perfect and the books in excellent order. At the head of one of the rooms the whole length portrait of George IV in regimentals. Since 1822 the church of the university appropriated as library and a very fine one it makes'.* However, she found the museum less impressive, noting that there was *'nothing very particular – several foetus in spirits, snakes, etc. etc. some skulls and a few stuffed birds and animals and south sea clothes, spears etc. – a dried man (with his feet gone) from part of the Hartz'*.

Anne spent the third day in Göttingen in bed.

In the bed all the day for my cold – literally in a state of solution. The bed over me as heavy as that under, and both the one and the other and my pillow were quite wet when I got up. Lying in bed is no gentle remedy in Germany – few hours longer and I should hardly have been about to stand, so excessive had been the perspiration.

Yet I felt my cold not much changed by it. All tendency to, or all feeling of sore throat was gone, and perhaps I breathed rather easily – but this was all. No occasion for washing – dried myself with a towel and lay on the sofa all the evening while my bed was dried. Had breakfasted in bed about 10 on boiled milk as usual. Dined on boiled milk and bread with some warm *compote de pommes*[37] and had a little boiled milk afterwards. Miss Ferral sat in the sitting room all day to be near me for fear I should want anything. Dined at 6 – left me at 9. Sat up a little looking over my map etc. Rainy day – F61° at 9 ½ p.m. Feel very weak, but my cold rather better tonight?

– 2 September 1833

She obviously felt better two days later because she '*incurred a cross just before getting up, thinking of Miss Walker*,' and after breakfast, set off from their inn, the König von Preussen, towards Einbeck.

---

37. *compote de pommes* (French): apple sauce

Chapter Five

Einbeck to Bremen

Einbeck, in Lower Saxony, was such a little-known town it did not warrant a mention in guidebooks of the nineteenth century. Even today, it is deemed unworthy to grace the pages of popular modern guidebooks. The town is, as the crow flies, sixty kilometres west of the summit of the Brocken in the Harz. Anne, still weak, unwell and oppressed with her cold, decided not to make the excursion to climb the Brocken. Perhaps it was a blessing in disguise. The Harz is Germany's most northerly range of mountains, and the Brocken, at 1,141 metres its highest summit. The mountains rise dramatically out from a level plain, and while summiteers would be rewarded on a clear day with a relatively nice view, the climate of the Harz is such that the hiker would invariably be enveloped in fog or rained upon.

However, what the Harz mountains may lack in Alpine dramatics, it makes up with some of Germany's oldest, most endearing villages which are tucked away in this region shared by three states: Lower Saxony, Thuringia and Saxony Anhalt.

I decided to stay the night in quaint little Einbeck and sought out the oldest, historical hotel I could find, hoping that I might perhaps chance upon an inn Anne might have stayed in, or stayed close to. I later found out she had spent the night at '*the Poste and White Swan, just opposite the great old Gothic (red sandstone) church*', and although there is a hotel called Der Schwan very close to the church, it was built in the early 1900s.

I was delighted when I entered Einbeck with its impressive collection of half-timbered houses from the sixteenth century, and its charming, landmark, historic town hall, with its three-pointed round towers. I was doubly delighted when I learnt that Einbeck brewed its own beer, called bock – an evolution of the word *oänpock* or *oänbock*, which the Bavarian accent mangled for Einbeck beer or rather, *Ainpöckische bier*. Bock beer, a bottom-fermented lager, has been brewed in Einbeck since the fourteenth century. Malty, toasty and just delicious overall, its reputation was such that in 1614, Hofbräuhaus, the court brewery of one of the oldest German noble families in Munich, enlisted the Einbeck brewmaster, Elias Pichler, to stylise their Munich brew after the popular north German beer. During the Thirty

Years' War in the seventeenth century, the resulting brew saved the lives of the Munich citizens when invading Swedes agreed not to destroy the city in exchange for 600,000 barrels of Hofbräuhaus beer.

My hotel room, for a negligible sum of €58, including breakfast, turned out to be a spacious rustic apartment in a timber-framed building dating back to the seventeenth century. Its creaky floorboards and wonky wooden stairs lent it a most endearing and enchanting personality. I could have stayed there very comfortably for a few days, exploring the region. The bedroom was large, bright and airy, and had its own lounge in the next room along with a dining area. The en-suite was about half the size of the entire apartment.

Einbeck might be small and almost forgotten, but its history is not unexciting. Apart from its contribution to German beer, it has a gruesome and fascinating history that would have very likely appealed to Anne. In July 1540 the city of Einbeck was nearly completely destroyed by a fire started by arsonists. Convicted of the crime, the ringleader, Heinrich Diek, was tortured to death while being publicly displayed in an iron cage, hung upon a tower just beyond the city gate. His body was left on display on the tower which became known as Diekturm. His remains were taken down only after ten long years and he was then finally buried. A replica cage now hangs on the prominent Diekturm on Reinserturmweg, unmissable as one enters the old town of Einbeck. The original cage is still on display in the town hall.

Anne's visit was brief, a mere sixteen hours. Her cold was not improving, her throat was sore and she had a *'great pain in the back'*. She would have liked to visit the *'great old Gothic (red sandstone church)'* which was said to contain some curiosities, but as the church was shut, she decided to push on to Hanover. '*I had no time to lose. Off from Einbeck, a good little wood town*'.

I myself left Einbeck in good spirits. Buoyed by the tiny, pretty, charming town, I followed Anne to Hanover, my car boot fuller with the addition of Einbecker beers.

Anne journeyed via Ammensen, Brüggen and Thiedenwiese to Hanover and my route did not stray too far from hers. Enchanted by the countryside and agricultural fields of this region, I had decided to shun the autobahn and drive at a more leisurely pace through small villages. Often, I would stop for a coffee in a petrol station by these quieter roads. The service was invariably warmer and the conversation more interesting. It was in such a petrol station, on my way to Hanover, that I met three women bikers who invited me to join them at their bar table. We made polite conversation about the weather, where we were going and why. They did not know who Anne Lister was and not wanting to make the conversation long or complicated, I said, 'She travelled a lot…'. As I was leaving, one of them asked me if I wanted to have a look at her bike. Ever polite, I said, '*Gerne*' (yet another efficient German word which means 'Yes, gladly, with pleasure'). We went outside to look at her high-powered BMW motorcycle and most of the technical specifications she described were beyond the limits of my comprehension of the German language. I summed up the conversation by simply saying, 'It sounds pretty powerful' and I conveyed what I hoped, was appreciation and knowledge.

She looked me in the eyes and said, 'Imagine feeling all that power between your thighs'.

There was a pause in the conversation, as we held each other's gaze. I could hear the whisper of the leaves, rustling on their branches. Whatever German I knew fled from my bewildered brain. In the absence of an appropriate response, I blurted out, 'Do you think it will rain?'

We shared a little awkward laugh and said our goodbyes. My embarrassment complete, I slunk back to my car with my tail between my legs. Then I drove off and collected my second speeding ticket of the journey within five kilometres of leaving the petrol station. Until that moment, I had been so proud that I had only received one speeding ticket on my way to Trier.

Anne's journey was much slower, and she covered the same distance, of approximately seventy-five kilometres to Hanover in seven hours, while I managed it in just a little more than an hour.

Hanover, the capital of the kingdom of Hanover, is situated on the banks of the Leine and is *'a very good town, and they say one of the gayest and pleasantest on the continent in winter'*. The dynastic union with the British monarchy was created in 1714 when Georg Ludwig of Hanover ascended the British throne as George I while concurrently ruling Hanover. This British-German union lasted until 1837 when Wilhelm IV died without leaving any descendants. In 1833 the royals' movements and going-ons were hot news, a point captured by Anne in her diary.

> *Lord Villiers gone to Magdeburg to see the revue on the 5th instante mense*[1] *– 2,500 men encamped there. The King of Prussia and Emperor of Russia will be there. Lord Villiers then return to England by Coblentz for a horse race on the 27th instante mense – leaves his brother here for six months to learn the language. The Duke of Cambridge will be back in 5 or 6 weeks and then there will be balls and parties.*
>
> – 6 September 1833

In a cruel twist of fate, Hanover's rich architectural heritage was nearly eradicated during the Allied bombing of World War II. Up to ninety percent of the city centre was destroyed. There are some landmarks that Anne

---

1. *instante mense* (Latin): of the current month

wrote about in her diary which have miraculously survived or have since been restored in the decades following the war. The Waterloo column, in a small park situated between the Leine and Ihme rivers, survived. So too did Leibniz's house and the monument dedicated to him, the Liebniz temple in Georgengarten. The Heerenhausen Palace and its gardens suffered extensive damage in World War II and were only recently reconstructed between 2009 and 2013. When Anne visited in September 1833, the area was an idyllic and pleasant place.

> *Went to the parade to see the Waterloo column[2] surmounted by a statue of Victory to the memory of all those Hanoverians killed at Waterloo. Handsome pediment and fluted stone column, each face of the pedestal covered by a large bronze plate with the names of all, officers and men, inscribed who were killed in the battle and at each corner, two of the canons taken (small with an N on each). Should have gone to the top for the view, but had not time.*
>
> *Thence along George Street (best part of the town) the old rampart now planted and a row of good houses on the town side, and thro' the double rows*

---

2. Waterloosäule, am Waterlooplatz, Hanover. Visitors are still allowed to ascend the column to the viewing platform at the base of the statue of Victory to this day.

of fine lime trees lining the fine wide road to Mount Brilliant (a wood built house but all whitened over). The nice little comfortable summer residence of the Duke and Duchess of Cambridge. Sauntered in the pretty little green park, thence straight forwards to Heerenhausen, the king's palace (both these places built by the Elector Ernest Augustus). Sauntered in the gardens in the old French style – long clipt hornbeam-hedges – fountain that shoots up the water (when playing) to 80 feet – some fine orange trees. Then saw the interior of the palace fitted up by George IV – his fine large full-length portrait by Sir William Lawrence there and a good copy of it belonging to the Duke of Cumberland, and a vulgar portrait of George IV when a young man, done by a German at Vienna. 3 or 4 rooms of the palace heavy with silk – a tolerably good comfortable house – merely some old family pictures.

– 6 September 1833

She walked through the king's stables and declared them '*good, but the stalls not eight feet wide, and wonder why Norcliffe[3] thought them so handsome (the handsomest he had ever seen) – nothing to compare to those at Chantilly*'. She entered the fourteenth-century Marktkirche, recording that she '*went into the handsome centuries old*

---

3. Thomas Norcliffe, Isabella Norcliffe's father.

Einbeck to Bremen

brick cathedral – Lutheran and pewed and benched. About the altar and pulpit much carved – galleries, fronts of, painted. Painted plafond within the groinings[4] *– enormous brick round columns, singular handsome old church'*. There, she looked about the town, *'very much struck with the very old, high pointed, Gothic, old gable ends of the houses in the old town'*. Wandering about town she came to the former home of mathematician and philosopher Gottfried Wilhelm Leibniz.

> *Where he lived and died, in Schmidt Street. Very handsome and well preserved (a print shop is one part of it) – the old town house (hotel de ville) is also in this fine old style, and well worth seeing – Leibnitz's monument, a bust under an Ionic peristyle of 12 columns (roofed) is near the Waterloo column and very handsome. The old town of Hanover very interesting.*
>
> – 6 September 1833

For one suffering so bad a cold, Anne was doing remarkably well, recording that she had been *'playing with Miss Ferral, very good friends. She sat on my knee tonight and has kissed me these three nights, but I do it all very properly'*.

---

4. A groin vault ceiling is formed by two barrel vaults intersecting at right angles. The result is four curving surfaces that draw the eye up and toward the center. The areas where the barrel vaults come together create ribs that add both strength and visual appeal.

It was my new friend, Frau 'Feel-the-power-between-your-thighs' who told me about Lister Meile (Lister mile) in Hanover. It was outside the old town, beyond the main train station. She said she did not know if it had anything to do with Anne Lister, but that I should check it out while there. I found out that it was established in the 1970s as a shopping street. The present Lister Meile is originally part of the highway from Hanover to Celle and likely named Lister due to its proximity to the district of List.

From Hanover, the landscape started to change as Anne continued her travels north westerly towards Bremen.

Dead flat to Neustadt[5] – entering the town cross old stone bridge over the Leine, muddy with the rain and now a goodish river, wide as the Ouse at the Manor Shore, York. Rain for the last hour (now 11 ¾ am) and strongish north east wind. Just after passing the bridge, large old brick church. Neustadt a small wood town – very little corn to Neustadt – and little or none afterwards.

Germany poor pasture, or heather, and here and there, a few whins[6] – very poor sandy land, or peat,

---

5. Neustadt am Rübenberge
6. whin: very spiny and dense evergreen shrub with fragrant golden-yellow flowers; common throughout western Europe

cocks[7] *of it here and there – like Les Landes in France – plain bleak ground – 2 or 3 pieces of fir plantation (Scotch). The other wood that we drove thro', birch.*

Niendorf[8] *small wood-built town but whitened or smeared over so the wood-work not so apparent, but well enough seen thro' on examination, as is the wood-work of Mount Brilliant near Hanover.*

Just out of the town pass old stone bridge over the good river Leine – very few villages after Herrenhausen, and those very small. Still heathery country but rather better than the last stage. Relieved by more patches of cultivation. Fields parted by alder or birch hedges growing on embankments. The road (everywhere wide) too hedged off with low alder or birch – before this in several places lined with poplars, some Lombardy.

– 7 September 1833

At Asendorf, Anne left Miss Ferral at the *gasthaus*[9] and '*in a small calêche and pair*[10] *(myself with the postilion and Thomas inside, that I might see the country)*' went to

---

7. cock: a small pile (as of hay or peat)
8. Nienburg
9. *gasthaus* (German): inn
10. *calêche* and pair: a light low-wheeled carriage with a removable folding hood, drawn by a pair of horses

Memsen *'to see the king's cream-coloured stud of brood mares'*.

However, Anne's enjoyment of Germany was dampened by Miss Ferral who was eager to get to Hamburg, where she intended to visit relatives from the noble von Qualen branch. It seemed as though all the intimacies of the previous days were unravelling. Anne reflected:

> *Miss Ferral so little thinking of my pleasure. I had said this morning, sorry for the delay, but really, I might have been a month longer but for her anxiety to get to Hamburg. She was sorry to have been de trop,[11] that I had said she was clearly enough, etc. etc.*
>
> *I civilly said I did not mean to say so, and slept or read and hardly spoke afterwards. If she was to be long delayed she thinks she would be mad, perhaps she is half so already. I have before felt gênée[12] now I do feel it thoroughly and shall be heartily glad to be rid of her. Said I did not think it right to take her when she was so tired – her German has served me very little. I must get a courier of some sort, a coachman and my own horses and be at less expense.*
>
> *– 7 September 1833*

---

11. *de trop* (French): too much
12. *gêné* (French): constrained or uncomfortable

Einbeck to Bremen

The next morning, in cloudy weather, they made their way towards Bremen. Anne noted the people and the landscape in which they travelled, *'the women generally in black, with very small cottage coarse-straw bonnets[13] covered with black riband[14] laid plain over – several enclosures, fields, hay but very poor peaty heather land, except where turned up – the alder or birch hedges and some small plantations of Scotch fir and some beech and birch woods make the country look richer – more cultivation today than yesterday – a little corn – (oats) potatoes and red cabbages for sourkraut[15]'*.

They entered Syke, *'a pretty little good scattered village amid orchards and gardens backed by a fine beech wood'*, and as soon as they departed, saw *'the four spires of Bremen, to the right, ahead'*. They crossed seven wooden bridges, over drains and ponds on soft ground, Anne observing *'nothing to be seen on either side but a low dead flat, goodish pasture stocked with young cattle, some cows and horses. The willow-hedged poplar or alder avenued road, so many drains, one might be in the best part of Holland'*.

Fifteen minutes after paying toll at the Bremen barrier, they arrived at the Hotel zum Lindenhof, situated in the main square, Domshof. The hotel, named for the linden trees that dotted the square, was situated at the far end

---

13. straw cottage bonnet: hat with an open face framing brim which is lined or bound to cover any raw edges
14. Archaic word for ribbon.
15. sauerkraut: finely sliced raw cabbage fermented through the process of lacto-fermentation

away from the town hall and cathedral of Bremen, then a prestigious hotel and restaurant district.

Bremen was special to me. It was one of the cities my dog, Ziggy, and I had explored together. We had dined in the Ratskeller, a vaulted, cavernous, traditional north German restaurant, situated in the cellar of the old town hall. The waiter was especially kind to Ziggy and brought him a large bowl of water and gave him a warm pet before bringing me my beer. Memories came flooding back of us strolling in the neighbourhood of Schnoor, Böttcherstraße and along the Weserpromenade. It was an emotional moment, my chest tightened and my eyes stung as I strolled along Am Dom towards the cathedral.

Along with a valet de place[16], Anne *'went to the fine large, old brick cathedral'*, the Dom Bremen. Mass was just over, and she explored the handsome Gothic cathedral, admired the *'large fine-looking organ filling up the west end'* and *'very handsome, richly carved pulpit'*. Then she entered the Bleikeller.

> *The crypt or vault and the 8 dried bodies, dried up like leather, like the bodies at Göttingen in the museum and at Blumenbach's. The oldest 400 years, a large old English countess – the last, a workman put in 48 years ago to see if the vault had still this inexplicable property of drying the bodies. Yes! He*

---

16. valet de place: person employed as a guide to transient travellers and strangers, usually available from the traveller's hotel or inn

is now just like the rest. There is a large old Swedish general and his young aide de camp[17]. A man who fell from his work on the top of the cathedral and broke open his neck and a man who died from a large cut in the arm, both these wounds very evident. There is an English major with half the hair on his head and a woman, all lying in large clumsy black coffins, the lids of which are all lifted up to shew the cadaver within – lying in cloth, yellow like mummy cloth, merely a middle cloth over the bodies – tho' the old countess had the cotton knitted gloves and a cap and stockings said to be those she was buried in.

– 8 September 1833

The Bleikeller is open to visitors at certain days of the week, depending on the season. I was lucky to be in the right place, at the right time when I followed Anne's trail to Bremen. I descended the few steps from the Bible garden, south of the main cathedral door, beyond the wrought iron gate and into the creepy, still, soft-lighted cellar. I was the first tourist of the day and alone in the crypt. As I contemplated the desiccated bodies, still in their coffins as Anne found them exactly 186 years ago, a raw tangible emotion of wonder and awe hit me: I was standing there and looking at the same things she saw. It

---

17. aide de camp: a military officer acting as a confidential assistant to a senior officer

was an indescribable feeling. My heart beat a little faster and there was an almost indiscernible tremble of my hands.

The mummified bodies were found by chance in 1698 when Arp Schnitger was building the organ[18] in the cathedral. The bodies were immaculately preserved as a result of the incredibly dry air in the crypt. The name Bleikellar arose from the fact that lead was stored in the east crypt (*blei* is the German word for lead). However, this had no effect on the mummification. In 1822, the mummies were moved from the east crypt (now the Room of Silence) to the coal cellar and have remained there since.

After examining the bodies, Anne walked about the town and *'went into one of the old houses with a large door, entering a sort of hall, taking up almost all the ground floor'*. She noted there were *'small rooms on each side and a sort of gallery on one side of the top and pictures on the other side above the 3 or 4 larger armoires*[19] *holding all the family stock of linens, plates, etc. etc. and the carriage (calêche) standing at the far end. The windows of the premier*[20] *light this hall and the little lodging rooms looking into it and at the end into*

---

18. Schnitger's organ was later replaced in the mid-nineteenth century by Johann Friedrich Schulze's.

19. *armoires* (French): cupboards

20. *premier* [*étage*] (French): first floor

the street. All above is grenier[21] *– was full of corn etc. and I was not to enter. What curious houses!'*

Bremen residents may have had curious houses, but Anne also noted there were *'some very rich people here'*. Bremen was an old prosperous Hanseatic city and it was always a little classy and well off. There is an old adage which compares three of the major German Hanseatic cities: *'Lübeck drinks, Hamburg eats and Bremen lives above its station'*. The typical old Bremen houses generally came in large versions and were home to wealthy merchants and captains. This fact was not lost to Anne, who observed:

> *The old ramparts turned into walks and gardens the old fosse*[22] *forming a pretty lake – very pretty, and all the new houses looking on to these. Neat and on the modern French or English plan, not more than 2 or 3 storeys at most. Neat and comfortable, not large houses – from 200 to 300 thalers a year rent or perhaps something more unfurnished. Some very rich people here. One merchant who sends out 150 ships per annum. No titre*[23] *people – four bürgermasters*[24] *and a president, which last, is changed every 6 months.*
>
> – 8 September 1833

---

21. *grenier* (French): attic, granary
22. fosse: a long, narrow trench especially in a fortification, moat
23. *titre* (French): a person of rank or claim to the throne
24. *bürgermeister* (German): mayor

Anne's tour of Bremen continued the next day. She visited the town hall and entered the Ratskeller and marvelled at the Bacchus barrel in the cellar.

> *Up at six but lay on the bed an hour – fineish, hazyish morning at both hours. F60° at 7 a.m. Breakfast at 8 ½ …*
>
> *Went to the fine old hôtel de ville[25] – exterior Gothic, finely carved. The handsomest I ever saw except that at Ypres. The ground floor a sort of maison de foire[26] – full of little shops. The premier[27], a very fine old Gothic lofty room, 105 by 18 paces of about 2 feet. I should think quite 18 paces high – ceiling boarded over the beam-like joists and painted (in stucco?) the old fashioned way.*
>
> *Below the ground floor is the famous Rosenkeller (or cellier officinal, government wine cellar) for the Rhine and Moselle wines sold by the senate. Some immense tonneaux[28] – one (the largest) containing 120 hogsheads[29] – a great Bacchus astride of a ton[30],*

---

25. *hôtel de ville* (French): townhall
26. *maison de foire* (French): fairground
27. *premier [étage]* (French): first floor
28. *tonneaux* (French): barrels
29. hogshead: a measure of capacity for wine
30. *ton* (French): barrel

and turn left into the cave[31] *with the Twelve Apostles i.e. 12 hogheads of wine. Got the prix courant*[32] *and bought a demie bouteille*[33] *of Johannisberg*[34] *of the year 1783 for fifteen good groschen*[35]*.*

– 9 September 1833

Wines have been stored and sold in the Ratskeller since it was built in 1405. It is one of the oldest wine cellars in Germany and home to the oldest cask wine of Germany, the Rüdesheimer from 1653. Bacchus, the god of wine and all things related to it, still sits astride its barrel. The twelve barrels of wine that Anne saw in Apostelkeller are each named after one of the apostles and still contain wines from the Rhine region dating back to the eighteenth century. In the 1800s in Germany, one hogshead was equal to approximately 286 litres[36]. The large wine barrel which Anne recorded as

---

31. *cave* (French): cellar
32. *prix courant* (French): current price
33. *demie bouteille* (French) half bottle
34. Johannisberg wines originated from the wine growing region of Rheingau in Hesse, Germany. The area grows predominantly the Riesling varietal.
35. *gute groschen* (German): German coin used as currency in the 1800s. 24 gute groschen was equal to 1 thaler, which in turn was approximately 3 shillings English
36. exactly 285 17/20 litres: Johann Friedrich Krüger: *Vollständiges Handbuch der Münzen, Maße und Gewichte aller Länder der Erde*. Gottfried Basse, Quedlinburg/Leipzig 1830, s. 126

containing 120 hogsheads, would have accommodated about 34,320 litres (7,549 imperial gallons), enough to fill approximately 45,760 standard wine bottles today. The Bacchus barrel is impressive, but not the largest in Germany. In comparison, the largest wooden wine barrel in the world, the leaky Heidelberg Tun, built in 1751 can hold a capacity of 220,000 litres.

I could not bring myself to revisit the Ratskeller while I was there in July 2019; the memories of Ziggy proved too overwhelming. However, I did trot up the tower of the Dom. Between April and October, visitors can climb the 265 steps to the top of the south tower of the Dom. The panoramic views are quite worth the effort, but are not easy to photograph due to the wire cage protecting the area from pigeons, or suicidal humans. The workout built up my appetite and I visited the Gaststätte Kleiner Olymp, a German restaurant that sets itself apart from the others by specialising in fish instead of pork, where I treated myself at dinner to several glasses of the local brew, Schnoor Bräu, and a North Sea plaice.

While Anne was in Bremen, she visited the Society Museum at the Domshof near her hotel. The museum was founded in 1783 and housed a natural history cabinet which included a female head preserved in spirits. Anne did not find the museum too exciting, but the preserved head did catch her attention.

Then half hour to the museum for which paid ½ thaler each for Miss Ferral and myself. Several people there – and the doctor explained all in German in spite of his saying he liked the English language. The fact was, he told nothing but the names of the things which were written on tickets affixed to each object and we left him and looked about and seeing nothing particular went away before his explanation was over. There was a pretty good collection of stuffed birds and the head in spirits, of a woman of Bremen hanged some time ago for poisoning two husbands and her children and servants.

– 9 September 1833

The head that Anne saw belonged to Gesche Gottfried, a serial killer who operated between 1813 and 1827. The 'Angel of Bremen', as she was called, killed fifteen people and made at least nineteen others sick[37]. Her earliest kill was her first husband, a lout and irresponsible drunkard who kept the company of prostitutes. Weary of him, to the point of disgust, she spread *Mäusebutter*, a mixture of arsenic and clarified butter for rats, on his bread for breakfast. He recovered from her first attempt, and so she added another dose to his soup. Four days later he died, his cause of death recorded as *'fever'*. Two years later

---

37. Meter, Peer – *Gesche Gottfried: Eine Bremer Tragödie*, Edition Temmen, 2016

she killed her ailing mother for being an inconvenience to her, employing the same modus operandi. A week following the death of her mother, she killed her young daughter, then the other.

This went on until her entire family, of which there were six members, was wiped out in 1816. Her immediate family now extinct, she turned her attention to others, including her second husband, a new flame, a maid, her friends, their children, a neighbour and many others, until she was arrested in 1828. Gottfried was executed, in the Bremen cathedral courtyard in 1831, not by hanging but by being beheaded with a sword. She was the last person to be publicly executed in Bremen. A *Spuckstein* – a spit-stone – was installed at the location where her head was separated from her torso. To this day, it remains in the Domplatz. Locals are said to spit on this stone to show contempt for Gottfried.

The head of Gottfried, still pickling in its yellowing preservatives was still in the museum when Anne passed through Bremen in 1839 on her way to Russia with Ann Walker. She '*had not time to go to see it at the museum*' but was told by her guide that the head '*was now so swollen in the spirit as not to be recognisable*'. The head of Gottfried was lost in the course of World War II, but one of the death masks which were made after her beheading is exhibited in the Focke Museum, Bremen near the Riensberger cemetery.

Einbeck to Bremen

I was glad to leave Bremen, not because I did not like the town – I loved it – but because I have a habit of running from grief rather than dealing with it. I could not leave Bremen fast enough and early the next morning, still not caffeinated and with my mind distracted, I picked up my third speeding ticket in a fifty kilometres per hour zone for driving at nearly sixty-five.

Chapter Six

Bremen to Copenhagen

*P*easants *mowing the short grass, sometimes mixed with a little short red clover. Cattle, a little hemp, some beans, all in stook[1], potatoes, sourcrout cabbages and buck wheat. People ploughing, 20 or 30 thatched farm cottages, barn and stable etc. under the same roof.*

– 9 September 1833

This was the scene of the idyllic countryside of Bremen as Anne Lister and her companions journeyed towards Ottersberg. In the small, scattered town of Ottersberg, their carriage rumbled through '*orchards and gardens, the people in the midst of the hay harvest*'.

---

[1]. A pile or bundle, especially of straw or sheaves of grain stacked to dry vertically in a rectangular arrangement at harvest time, obsolete since the mid-twentieth century.

After having travelled five hours from Bremen, they stopped for the night at Rotenburg, a quaint, little town Anne admired, with picturesque gable-ended houses, and street *'like a Parisian boulevard'* lined with *'lime trees, pollarded[2] and clipt flat and thin like walls as in France'*. As Elysian as the scene was, Anne was disappointed with her dinner at the *gasthaus*. There was *'only a larded hare, not well cooked, potatoes and bread and cheese'* and the worst scenario ever, *'no beer to be had'*.

The next day, it was obviously still heavy on her mind as she reiterated the fact in her diary entry, noting *'good beds and pretty comfortable in spite of the bad supper last night and no beer to be had'*. Her friendship with Miss Ferral also seemed less than perfect. Miss Ferral *'said we parted very different from what we began. I had been not the same person these last three days – had been out of humour. I laughed it off, would not allow it or merely made a joke of it. Shall be too happy to get rid of her. She does me no good and is very stupid and odd'*.

From Rotenburg, Anne and her party proceeded to Harburg where she took a steamer on the Elbe to Hamburg.

---

2. Pollarding is a method of pruning that keeps trees and shrubs smaller than they would naturally grow. It is normally started once a tree or shrub reaches a certain height, and annual pollarding will restrict the plant to that height.

Bremen to Copenhagen

> *On board in the carriage at 3 49/.. Fine river 2 or 3 yards broad, but have to go up the river a good way. The great boat bridge the French constructed here is destroyed. Under weigh at 4 – one other carriage (a calêche) on board. We close to the chimney and much incommoded by steam on setting off and arriving. Our forward view spoilt by the calêche in which 4 Germans, papa and mama and their daughter and her betrothed. The two young people a good specimen of German sentiment – looking most sweet on each other and absolutely kissing at intervals; she in the carriage with mama and he standing on the step.*
>
> – 10 September 1833

They navigated the river to arrive at the quay in Hamburg, where their carriage was pulled from the boat onto land by twelve men. A pair of horses was ready for them and immediately hitched to the carriage and they set off to the Hotel Stadt London which was recommended by Miss Ferral. The hotel was nearly full and they accommodated Anne and Miss Ferral in a double-bedded room. Sharing a room was uncomfortable for Anne, who could not use the chamber *'pot before Miss Ferral'* and had to use the public restrooms. Her discomfort was exacerbated when she was compelled to ask a young lad to show her the way, *'went thro' all the people, the garçon[3] shewing the way and opening the very door for me'.*

The necessary attended to, Anne and Miss Ferral spent a quiet night, *'sat at her bedside till eight and after, talking and occasionally kissing her very gently and properly. She nothing loth'*.

Hamburg was another city I had visited with Ziggy. I was keen to leave it behind and decided not to stay the night. I parked in the city centre and wandered in the old town and strolled around the Jungfernstieg, the promenade which ran along the western end of the Binnenalster. The word Jungfernstieg translates to maiden's path, a reference to the young maidens who were paraded there by their parents on Sunday afternoons in the quest for a suitable husband. But instead of chaste virgins, Anne ran into *'a highly painted lady'*. She must have then investigated this for she confirmed there were *'7,000 ladies in Hamburg – each pay 2 marks a month to government'*. It was likely she obtained all this information from her guide or valet de place who may very well have himself, on occasion, partaken of the sinful midnight pleasures of these women. But she did not credit him in her diary, which leaves room for conjecture. In the 1890s, there were four thousand sex workers in the city, and today there are around ninety brothels with an estimated 2,500 prostitutes operating

---

3. *garçon* (French): lad, boy, chap

in Hamburg[4]. The modern sex worker's tax return is more complicated today than it was in the nineteenth century. Commercial fornication is classified as a trade by the tax office. Accordingly, in addition to income tax, sales and trade tax must also be paid. The tax rate is progressive, which means that the more revenue a sex worker generates, the higher the tax. A sex worker generating an annual income of about €55,000 would be obliged to pay twenty-seven percent income tax, nineteen percent sales tax and 3.5 percent trade tax on profits.

Anne and her little group settled into Hamburg for two full days, which allowed Miss Ferral to visit her relatives, the von Qualens in Altona while Anne took in the sights of Hamburg. She strolled along the Jungfernstieg, studied the plants in the botanic gardens, and visited the churches of St Michael, *'large and handsome'*; St Peter, *'large, handsome organ filling up the west end of the nave'*; and St Nicholas, *'handsome, richly carved, painted white organ with lead-like pipes'*. She also mounted the old ramparts of the Stintfang – *'a fine view along it'* – and wandered the streets.

> *Walked about, crossing the different bridges over the waters that run along several of the streets of the old*

---

[4]. Stiftung Historische Museen Hamburg

> *town. One of these in which a great many brewers live, called Brewers Street – the cranes alongside the water with penthouses over them have a singular appearance. Small vessels come up these waters and load and unload at the doors, remind me of Rotterdam and Amsterdam. Not like Venice because there is a paved street way on each side the water there all along the Elbe.*
>
> – 12 September 1833

In her wanderings, she browsed in book shops, print and stationery establishments and toy stores. At the Hamburg *fête*[5], she '*paid 8 schillings for my ticket to Cirque Horsemanship – rope dancing, extraordinary balancing of balls and leaping etc. etc. Men of colour, probably Indian jugglers but speaking German. Exceedingly amused there for above half hour*'.

In the evenings, Miss Ferral and Anne had dinner together and their little dance of flirting and confounding courtship continued.

> *Glad enough to see her but should do very well without her and shall be glad enough in reality to be without her? She sat on my knee this evening. I tell her she is not ugly and she is well enough inclined to flirt with me but I am very prudent.*
>
> – 11 September 1833

---

5. *fête* (French): festival

Sat an hour at her bedside talking foolishly enough for she was not ready till near ten, and I seeing the room swept etc. was delayed – she saying I was a great fidget and she could not live [with] me.

– 12 September 1833

On the eve of their departure from Hamburg, Miss Ferral's little rat of a dog hammered the final nail into her coffin.

Stood talking to her half an hour – her little dog had made water in the bedroom and on Eugénie's bed. Could not sleep for its snoring last night. Sick of it. Could not get another room so put my bed in the sitting room, on the sofa and three chairs. Wish I had done so before.

– 12 September 1833

They departed the next day just after noon, Anne grumbling, '*should have been comfortable enough without Miss Ferral and her snoring disagreeable little dog*'. Anne had found the Alten Stadt expensive, but the proprietor, Georg Hillert very civil.

Anne's hotel in Hamburg, the Hotel zur Alten Stadt London, burnt down in the Great Fire of 1842 and then the Hôtel de Russie and Sillem's Bazaar was built on the site. The site was then repurposed to become the Hamburger Hof in 1883 which was then the best hotel in the city. It went through some restoration and improvements after a fire and World War II, and now commands a prominent frontage on the Jungfernstieg as an office building and shopping arcade.

Anne's relationship with Miss Ferral soured further as they travelled to Ahrensburg. Anne had agreed to stop in the village in order for Miss Ferral to visit another set of relatives at Schloss Ahrensburg, a moated castle which served as the summer residence of the von Schimmelmanns. Before they left Hamburg, Mr Hillert had forewarned Anne about the horrific conditions of the next stage of her journey. The road they were to take was in a dire condition and fourteen kilometres out of their way to Lübeck. Anne sat in her carriage and fumed even as they journeyed just half a mile from Hamburg.

> *The road became so vilely bad, I never in my life saw anything like it for a gentleman's carriage. A boulder stone pavement all in holes – terrible. I expected breaking down and sat in mute despair finding it not safe to abuse the road as Miss Ferral seemed inclined to think I was blaming her for it, and when she heard at the inn how bad it was never thought of offering to go in another carriage but talked only of the 'must set her down there' – at last in about ½ or ¾ hour we got off this miserable pavé into the deep-rutted sand and worse than any cart road in England, and thought this a god send.*
>
> *– 13 September 1833*

It took them three hours to travel the twenty-five kilometres from Hamburg to the village of Ahrensburg at an average speed of about eight kilometres per hour or five miles per hour. When they finally pulled up at La Poste in the *'good, pretty village'* of Ahrensburg, Miss Ferral strode off on her own to the castle less than a kilometre away. As Anne set about ordering horses for the onward journey, she met a man whom she assumed was the von Schimmelmann family's butler. He invited Anne for dinner at the castle and was soon *'ushered into a hall, the whole depth of the château, into which opened all the rooms'*. There, she found *'the Comtesse Schimmelmann[6], a sallow, sickly, interesting widow and her mother, old Comtesse Blücher[7], a nice agreeable old gentlewoman and Miss Ferral'*.

Dinner was a formal affair round a large, bountiful table.

> *Soup, then a large round dish with about a dozen pigeons. I thought they were, but they were too white and more like small partridges or what? These, Comtesse Schimmelmann cut each into two (or 2 or 3 of them into 3) and they were handed round with small roast-under-meat potatoes and boiled small*

---

6. Fanny Sophie von Blücher of Altona (1797-1835), widow of Friedrich Joseph Schimmelmann who had recently died in January 1833, aged 45.

7. Marie Barbara (Manon) Abbestée (1770-1852), wife of Conrad Daniel von Blücher-Altona (1764-1845).

cut red cabbage. Then came a dish of compote of apple done over with bread crumbs, and was handed round. Then dessert (a melon) handed round, some pears and plums and voilà tout[8] – but all very good and comfortable. Two manservants in black, one with, one without épaulettes[9]. We had good vin de Bourgogne on the table at dinner the servant going round and filling everyone's glass.

– 13 September 1833

Anne was impatient to head to Lübeck and after dinner they said their goodbyes. In private, Sophie Ferral was conciliatory and contrite for the inconvenience she had put Anne through, but yet still stroppy, as Anne noted:

Said she was sorry she had come with me. I civilly remonstrated. She said (out of sorts) perhaps she did not understand English, I expressed as before (just out of Hanover) my anxiety for her to have an agreeable journey, my sorrow etc. etc. and did not utter many words more. On leaving me she just kissed me and said she hoped I was not angry with her. I said, 'Oh no! Why should I?' and thus we parted. I heartily glad to get rid of her and her dog [even] if I cannot speak one word of German. She cannot do much and

---

8. *voilà tout* (French): that is all
9. Ornamental shoulder piece to distinguish insignia of rank.

has always been too careless to exert herself to help me beyond the mere thing I asked her to say.

She says her aunt's impatience sinks into nothing compared with mine. She would not travel with me on any account and could not live with me. I hope she will never be tried.

– 13 September 1833

Anne could not leave Miss Ferral quickly enough. They would meet up again, several days later, in Lübeck before they travelled together to Travemünde for the steamer to Copenhagen. Anne had a bone-shaking yet peaceful journey to Bad Oldesloe, observing that *'the women in Holstein wear men's beaver hats'*. Bad Oldesloe was approximately twenty kilometres from Ahrensburg, and where she spent a quiet night reading and had boiled milk with good bread and butter. *'What a luxury to be alone. I shall not wish for a companion again in a hurry'*.

Twelve minutes to nine the next morning, Anne and her servants set off. The landscape to Lübeck, less than twenty-five kilometres away unfolding before her.

Good land all about here. Oak, hornbeam, hazel, maple and occasionally sauf[10] and willow hedges all along the road sides (with occasionally lilacs intermixed here as elsewhere ever since Hanover.

---

10. sauf (sic): saunf, fennel

> *The road still bad – granite boulder stone pavé, rough but less so than yesterday. Our road lies all along the Trave, its banks very low and full almost to the brim.*
>
> *A nice green low valley all the way to Lübeck. Smallish-hedges as in England – good pasture and grass land, not very much corn. Nice farming country and neat good husbandry. Nicely wooded, just like England. Good cattle and a few sheep. Good villages and farmsteads, brick and wood-built as everywhere – straw-thatched or tiled. Nothing wanted but good roads.*
>
> – 14 September 1833

The roads that Anne had been complaining about were notorious for being the worst in Europe in the 1800s. In fact, they had been pronounced as a disgrace to any civilised country. Beyond Hamburg, the Duchy of Holstein began at the town of Wandsbek. Though a member state of the German Confederation since 1815, its duke was the Danish king, and thus governed by the Danish state. The selfish policy of the king of Denmark kept its roads towards Lübeck and the east in an execrable condition in the hope of compelling travellers and goods to pass through the Øresund, where they must pay a toll to him. His other strategy was in making Kiel, less than a hundred kilometres north of Hamburg and on a good road, the port of embarkation on the way to St Petersburg, discouraging trade and travel to Lübeck[11], which was an independent city-state between 1226 to 1937.

The best route from Hamburg to Lübeck would have been via Schönberg, approximately halfway between the two cities. Anne's route via Ahrensburg and Bad Oldesloe would have put her on a horrendous bone-jolting track that could have easily ruined her carriage. Most of the routes were sandy tracks marked by wheels in the deep sand, interspersed with large boulder stones, laid as if to inflict more suffering upon already despondent travellers, and a goods wagon sometimes required eleven horses to pull a full load.

The postmaster at Bad Oldesloe had compelled Anne to take four horses for her flat stage to Lübeck, and said *'it did not depend on the number of persons, my carriage or coach, and he could even oblige me to take six horses'*. Even with four horses, it took Anne an hour and five minutes to travel one German *meile*, equivalent to seven and a half kilometres. She arrived in Lübeck, passing under the city gate nearly three and a half wretched hours after leaving Bad Oldesloe. She must have nearly wept in relief at the much improved conditions of the roads of the free city of Lübeck after those of Holstein.

---

11. Murray, John – *A Handbook for Travellers on the Continent*, 2nd edition, section V, published 1838

It was in Lübeck when I decided that a trip to the laundromat may be prudent. I was soon heading over the body of water called the Fehmarn Belt into Denmark, and as I could understand the operating instructions a whole lot better in German than in Danish, I braved a laundromat on the outskirts of town. As I sat opposite the dryer watching my clothes spin in soporific circles, I was envious that Anne had not needed to do any laundry herself till the ripe age of forty-nine. However, I did not share the same outrage she experienced on a fateful Tuesday, 21 July 1840, between eight and twenty to ten in the morning, '*Washing! At the run of water near the house – chemise and waist*[12] *– first time in my life*'. She did however, manage to '*get them tolerably clean, and dried them in the sun*[13]'. It took me nearly just as long to figure out how to work the machines in the laundromat and then put my clothes through the washing and drying cycles.

My own washing done, I entered the old town of Lübeck via the Holstentorplatz, which skirted alongside the Holstentor – the same charming, tremendous redbrick city gate Anne's carriage rumbled under after she crossed the Puppenbrücke. The Holstentor, which served both as a form of defence and of prestige, is a spectacular piece of architecture now that it has been

---

12. Article of clothing for women and girls, covering the body from the neck to the waist.
13. 21 July 1840 – WYAS SH:7/ML/E/24/0160

restored. It was built between 1464 and 1478 along the lines of Dutch models. Measuring over twenty metres, its two towers, connected by a central structure with a gable roof, commands awe as one passes beneath the massive structure into ancient Lübeck.

In 1833, the neglected towers were unevenly subsided into the marshy ground and by 1863 were an appalling sight. With a majority of just one single vote, the city parliament decided to restore the gate instead of demolishing it and began extensive restoration efforts. It was not until seventy years later that the subsidence could be stopped. The most recent renovations were carried out between 2004 and 2006 when the slate roof, terracotta frieze and parts of the brickwork were replaced.

The Puppenbrücke, a *'good, very pretty, six arched stone bridge (statues at each end) over the Trave'*, was the first stone bridge in Lübeck, constructed between 1770 and 1772. In 1774, the city council decided to adorn the bridge with eight statues, an equal number of male and female deities of symbolic significance, and four vases representing values such as diligence and thrift. The bridge was replaced in 1907, but the statues that Anne saw were saved and are displayed in the inner courtyard of the St Anne's Museum at St Annen Straße, Lübeck.

I spent a wonderful afternoon, blessed with blue skies and a strong sun, sitting and reading on the green in front of the Holstentor, marvelling at the structure. I was in awe that Anne too had been here, observing *'the old brick Porte de Holstein[14] very handsome. Reminds me of the Porte Noire à Trêves[15]. The front towards the town is quite in that style and has two towers too, but with pointed flêches[16] springing from them'*.

I had planned to spend two days in Lübeck and for the first time since leaving home, I had a leisurely afternoon. Moreover, I had not travelled to this part of Germany before and I just wanted to soak in the atmosphere. Lübeck was enchanting. A UNESCO World Heritage Site, its old town was an absolute delight to wander in, and included a treasure trove of ancient architecture dating back to its Hanseatic roots, old narrow cobbled-stone streets and impressive churches.

My first port of call after lazing in front of the Holstentor was the Petrikirche. Built between 1227 and 1250, it was expanded in the fifteenth and sixteenth centuries into a five-naved Gothic hall church. There is hardly a better view of Lübeck than from the top of the tower of Petrikirche. The fifty-metre high viewing platform affords sweeping views across Lübeck and the surrounding area. On a clear day, one can even see as far as the Baltic Sea.

---

14. *porte de...* (French): gate of...
15. Porta Nigra in Trier which Anne visited on 23 August 1833
16. *flêches* (French): arrows

Then, retracing my steps north, I walked through the old market place, Markt, to the Rathaus, a town hall sometimes described as a *'fairy tale in stone'*. Built between 1442 and 1517, this was the location in which delegates of the Hanseatic League held their meetings. From there, I headed to the Marienkirche, just around the corner from the Rathaus. The Gothic Marienkirche is the third largest church in Germany and was an ambitious project by the magistrate and merchants of Lübeck in the thirteenth century. In just eighty years, they created a soaring Gothic basilica of enormous dimensions. The vault spans the impressive nave at a height of 38.5 metres and the twin spires are 125 metres high. The basilica serves as a model for the Gothic brick style of churches in the Baltic region and costs the city €130,000 to maintain each year.

Anne was also similarly impressed with the church and attended mass there. Normally sleeping through mass, she found the service interesting enough to stay awake the entire time.

> *Out at 9 – went to St Mary's. The service had begun. Paid one schilling for my chair in the midst of the nave – all women there and in the pews. The men stood along the aisles and behind and as they could, perhaps in the galleries, could not look about much – too crowded.*

> *I got there at 9 10/.. and the service not over till 10 ½ – they were all singing (some of the congregation near me badly enough) when I went in and for about 10 minutes after. Then the priest got into the pulpit, seemed to pray a little, then gave a long sermon, (quietly delivered) then read the gospel. Then singing again and done – in the midst of the sermon, men went about with cups at the end of long shafts, begging and all seemed to put in a schilling or 2 – so should I, but the cup did not quite reach me.*
>
> *Never saw a more attentive congregation. The priest stopped a few seconds 3 or 4 times in his sermon and then all the people continued to blow noses and cough. Nothing of either at any other times. Never stood but once for a minute or two, while, as I suppose, the priest gave his blessing after his sermon.*
>
> – 15 September 1833

The Marienkirche was also home to two noteworthy attractions. The frieze of the Dance of Death, painted in 1463, and the astronomical clock, constructed in 1405. Anne remarked on both in her diary on 16 September, recording, '*The famous Danse Macabre or Danse des Morts par Holbein, in the sacristy – singular picture. Very good. Each Death in a different attitude and one between each pair of people*'.

Bremen to Copenhagen

The frieze, painted by Bernt Notke (not Hans Holbein nor Lucas van Leyden) conveyed the grim message that we will all perish, whatever our status or importance.

Lübeck's Danse Macabre was particularly intricate and special because it included the landscape and landmarks of Lübeck in the background. Due to its popularity, there are many surviving lithographs and black and white photographs. Unfortunately, the frieze was destroyed in 1942 when Allied forces bombed Lübeck. In the 1950s, two stained-glass windows that pay tribute to the lost Danse Macabre were installed in the Marienkirche. Anne was so taken with the frieze that she bought a print of it at the shop on Breite Straße which runs north alongside the church towards the city gate, Burgtor.

The astronomical clock that Anne saw suffered the same fate during World War II and the little of what survived is now homed in St Anne's Museum.

> *The clock struck at twelve, and seven instead of twelve apostles came out at one door and went in at another, having turned and bowed ridiculously to the Virgin and Child in passing – the other five apostles lost or out of order.*
>
> – 16 September 1833

The parading figures of the original clock were meant to represent the reverential obeisance of the seven Prince-Electors from the Holy Roman Empire of the German

Nation, not the apostles as Anne was led to believe. In the 1960s, a new and simpler version of the astronomical clock was built by Paul Behrens, a local clockmaker. It was installed in the Danse Macabre Chapel, to the east of the northern transept.

Anne visited the Domkirche too, which was said to be built on the spot where Henry the Lion, while hunting, pursued a stag that had a crucifix between its horns. According to Anne, the deer was so beautiful that Henry the Lion ordered it be turned loose and that no one else was to shoot it. Behind the altar, in one of the chapels was the renowned Passion of Our Saviour painting dated 1471. Unfortunately, this masterpiece did not quite meet Anne's approval.

> *In the Chapel de Greverode, so called because given by him, is the famous picture finished in 1471 of the Passion and Death of Jesus Christ by Jean Hemling, a disciple of Albert Dürer – the tears on the Virgin's face very good. The worst part of the picture is the body of Notre Sauveur[17] when taken from the Cross – is too flexible – too little like death.*
>
> *– 16 September 1833*

Here in Lübeck, I channelled my inner Lister and 'trespassed' in the private courtyards of Füchtingshof

---

17. *Notre Sauveur* (French): Our Saviour

and Glandorps Gang. These small, but cute and well-kept private courtyards are accessible only at certain hours of the day. At the height of the Hanseatic period, Lübeck's prosperity attracted numerous artisans and craftsmen which resulted in a surge of demand for housing. To rectify the problem cheaply and quickly, tiny single-storey buildings were built in the large courtyards of existing homes, made accessible via similarly tiny, narrow walkways. These houses have been preserved for their historical value and are now private residences. In the seventeenth century, through the last will and testament of Lübeck merchant and councillor, Johann Füchting, Füchtingshof was established as free housing for widows and orphans. Even today, the homes there are rented to single women in need, with the rent level below that of the market rate.

In Anne's wanderings of Lübeck, she not only took in the sights and learnt of the history of these fascinating landmarks, but also of exciting and interesting news within the town, including cholera, a favourite topic of the 1830s.

> *My guide had the cholera last June or July. Twice – first time 3 days – second 6. Was seized at midnight with violent cramps in his legs (calves) and arms and in half hour could not stand straight. Oppression at the chest, could scarce breathe, perpetual thirst, just about the tops of his nails blue but nowhere else. Got*

out of bed, took hot thé de Tilleul[18] *directly. And after the third drink, a little rhum and sugar in it. At last this threw him into a perspiration and did him good. The smell of the perspiration intolerable – like the worst putridity. In the morning put on dry linen and got out of bed. I think this saved him, this and not being afraid but for four months after, the pains returned every night at midnight when he was in bed. Afraid to lie down, not so bad when up but the pains were gradually less and less.*

When once recovered, felt lighter and better than he was before. Did not eat anything for some time and when he did begin to eat felt unwell after it at first. Friction with something soft (flannel) is the best thing. Does not believe it infected – it is the air – yet it was a stranger that was the first victim here. Died in an hour. He seems to believe there are 10 cases of it in the town now. 1,600 died of it here – all buried in the country we passed a little way out of the town.

Cholera patients to be buried in 24 hours but to have a hand cut off first to see if dead – some of the dead blue, some not. Knows nothing of the marble

---

18. Tea from the infusion of Linden leaves, valued by Germans for its restorative properties. Nowadays the tea is made with its flowers, but traditionally, the leaves were used to lower fever and treat colds, nasal congestion, insomnia, anxiety and other ailments.

coldness of the tongue but the corpse, instead of being stiff as in common cases, is quite mou (soft). The eyes sunk (lost) in the head in the course of an hour. The smell of the clothes during the perspiration quite horrible – ditto the smell of the excrement, but the moment after death, the perspiration[19] being stopt, the perspiration ceases. Fright is generally fatal.

– 16 September 1833

Anne spent a blissful three days in Lübeck without Sophie Ferral, but eventually that was to end and it was time to leave for the port of Travemünde. '*Changed my dress and all ready to be off at one. Miss Ferral arrived from Ahrensburg at 12 ¾ – somehow or other, this detained me till 1 ½, at which hour off from the Stadt Hamburg at Lübeck. Had been very comfortable and well satisfied with everything – a very good reasonable hotel*'.

I myself left Lübeck early on a rainy Friday morning. I too was heading to Travemünde to the old port where Anne had boarded her steamer to Copenhagen. I wanted to see it before I continued my journey north to Puttgarden to board my own ferry to Rødbyhavn in Denmark. The ferries at Travemünde no longer travel to Copenhagen, but to ports in Russia, Sweden, Finland, Estonia and Latvia. I could have crossed the Fehmarn Belt from Rostock into Gedser, but the sea journey

---

19. Anne may have intended to write 'respiration'.

between Puttgarden and Rødby was considerably shorter and I wanted to pop into Gavnø Castle on my way to Copenhagen. The castle, according to the *Visit Calderdale* website, was used for scenes in one of the episodes of *Gentleman Jack*. I also heard that they brewed their own beer.

I arrived in Travemünde and parked near the old lighthouse. This lighthouse, the Alter Leuchtturm, would have been the same that guided ships in and out of the port of Travemünde when Anne travelled. The round brick tower, which can still be seen on Leuchtenfeld, dates from 1539. After almost 450 years of uninterrupted service, the beacon of hope for many a sailor began a well-earned retirement in 1972. The lighthouse is the oldest in Germany and is now a museum. On arriving at Travemünde, Anne first supervised her carriage being loaded onto the *Frederik den Sjette* (*Frederick VI*), the steamer which chugged to Copenhagen every Saturday evening at seven o'clock from Kiel and every Tuesday evening at six from Travemünde.[20] At seeing the lighthouse at the port, Anne of course had to ascend it.

Went to the top of the phare[21] *– 60 brick steps and about five ladders of 15 steps each. Fine view of the river – the Baltic, the town, and very pretty baths*

---

20. Brown, Son & Ferguson – *The Nautical Magazine: A Journal of Papers on Subjects Connected with Maritime Affairs*, January 1833, p. 361
21. *phare* (French): lighthouse

and boarding-house with its pretty straw-thatched additional boarding house and stabling and nice little grounds in front.

– 17 September 1833

When I visited, it was too early to enter. Instead, I walked around the old port and admired the brick lighthouse from the outside.

Anne's steamer, the *Frederik den Sjette*, was the first Danish-built steam vessel. Built in 1830 in the shipyard of Jacob Holm & Sønner in Christianshavn, Copenhagen, it had a wooden hull reinforced with a copper skin and was equipped with an eighty-horsepower steam engine capable of cruising at a sedate eight knots. The boat started plying the waters in 1831 and was appointed with an onboard restaurant, sixty beds and five elegant comfortable cabins to cater to a capacity of 110 passengers; seventy-four in first class, and the rest in second[22]. Anne's sea journey of 140 nautical miles took between sixteen and eighteen hours. In contrast, my significantly shorter sea journey from Puttgarden across the Fehmarn Belt to Rødbyhavn took only forty-five minutes. My ferry, the Dutch-made *Scandlines FS Deutschland*, had five diesel engines capable of producing 15,840 kilowatts of power,

---

22. Museet for Søfart, Helsingør – *Handels- og Søfartsmuseet, Jahrbuch Søfartshistorie Danmark*, published 1950

an equivalent of 21,536 horsepower, with a service speed of 18.5 knots.

Anne enjoyed a mutton chop at the nearby inn called Stadt Hamburg then *'went on board the steamer exactly at 6 p.m'*. She was relieved when Miss Ferral immediately met an old acquaintance onboard, Madame Hage. It seems that, Miss Ferral's absence in Lübeck did not make Anne's heart any fonder of her, remarking *'lucky, thought I, I shall get comfortably rid of her. I had said to myself several times in the carriage I thought her the most disagreeable girl I ever saw and how heartily glad I should be to get rid of her'*.

At any rate, Anne attempted to settle down for the night after ambling about the 127-foot long boat restlessly for forty-five minutes until quarter past nine in the evening.

> *Then went to my carriage for the night. Lay across it with my feet up my travelling bag. Pretty comfortably till perhaps between 12 and 1 or an hour later. Dozing or slumbering, then sick about every quarter hour till 8 or 9 in the morning.*
>
> – 17 September 1833

Poor Anne, she never did get her sea legs.

Chapter Seven

Denmark

The Danes appear to be a kind-hearted and friendly people; enraged as they still are, and it must be owned not without just cause, at the treatment they experienced at our hands in 1807, and which still rankles in their hearts, though 30 years have since elapsed, they are still courteous and obliging to the English traveller. Though, in their arsenal they still preserve with jealous anxiety, a shell thrown into the capital during the bombardment, and on which they have inscribed 'English Friendship', and though no opportunity is lost of telling you how lofty their towers were, and how beautiful their churches before that fatal day, and the ready answer to every question for new curiosities is, that the English destroyed them, yet the enmity which now subsists is rather national than directed against individual Englishmen.

– *General View of Denmark, A Handbook for Travellers in Denmark, Norway, Sweden and Russia.* John Murray, Albemarle Street, London. 1839 edition

The honest summary of local sentiment towards the English alluded to the Battle of Copenhagen 1807, between 15 August and 7 September. The British were ruthless in their goal of neutralising the Danish navy which had allied with Napoleon. Fearful that a *'maritime league against Great Britain to which Denmark and Sweden and Portugal should be invited or forced to accede'*[1], the British naval fleet bombarded Copenhagen mercilessly between 2 and 5 September 1807. Over a thousand buildings were damaged[2]. On 5 September, their city in ruins, the Danes surrendered and turned over their fleet and naval stores to the British.

Denmark in 1833 was a lot calmer. The Danish state bankruptcy of 1813 and the agricultural crisis of the 1820s were behind them and prosperity was slowly returning. The 1830s also witnessed the Golden Age, when literature, arts and philosophy flourished in Denmark. Despite bumps along the way to their Elysian ideal – the First Battle of Copenhagen in 1801, followed by the Second Battle of Copenhagen of 1807 and the loss of Norway to Sweden in 1814 – the culture in Copenhagen continued to bloom. Ballets were being choreographed by the ballet maestro, August Bournonville, Bertel Thorvaldsen was busy chipping away at his marble masterpieces in

---

1. Canning to Gower, 22 July 1807, in A.N. Ryan. *Documents Relating to the Copenhagen Operation, 1807*, in N.A.M. Rodger, ed., *The Naval Miscellany* vol. 5 (London: Naval Records Society, 1984), 307

2. Vibæk, Jens – *Politiken Dansmarkshistorie*, vol. 10 p. 292 (1964)

Rome, Søren Kierkegaard was deep in thought and Hans Christian Andersen conjured fairy tales which went on to enthral children and adults even into the twenty-first century.

Anne's arrival into Copenhagen was a quiet affair. Mr de Hagemann, the husband of her friend, Lady Harriet de Hagemann, took a little boat to Anne's steamer which was anchored in the Copenhagen harbour. On board, he helped to make arrangements for her carriage and then took her to his house where she sat with Lady Harriet while Mr de Hagemann escorted Sophie Ferral to the Blücher's. A little while later, Lady Harriet accompanied Anne to the Hotel Royal and, when she was sure Anne was comfortable, left her to her own devices. Anne *'lay down at 2 ½ (having no travelling bag and journal book and nothing to do) till 4'*.

My own arrival into Denmark was a little more hectic. Rushing for the ferry in Puttgarden after my little saunter around Travemünde, my car hit speeds exceeding 215 kilometres per hour. The autobahns in Germany today are nothing like the sad state of roads on which Anne had to travel in Holstein. I embarked the nine thirty ferry with a few minutes to spare. The waters were kind to me. I was a little apprehensive about a ferry journey across the Belt as I am inclined to be sick when in motion on a turbulent sea or in the air. I was armed with motion sickness tablets, but had decided against them as the journey was less than an hour and because they may have made me drowsy. Instead, I distracted myself by browsing in what posed as the duty free shop and being outraged at the price of beer.

Fresh off the ferry, I set the GPS for Gavnø Castle and eagerly set off. It was my first trip into Denmark and I was keen to explore. I observed that the landscape of Denmark along the E47 was one continual golden sea of barley and wheat. It was incredibly picturesque and pastoral. About fifty minutes from Rødby, I took the turn-off for Næstved and soon crossed the little stone bridge onto the immaculate grounds that was Gavnø island.

Gavnø Castle's foundation was established more than six hundred years ago. In 1737, its collection of paintings, the largest private collection in Northern Europe was begun by Count Otto Thott. He was renowned as a book collector too and his private library was built to house approximately 200,000 books. I took my time to walk in the gardens, then visited the fifteenth-century chapel before taking the tour of the picture gallery and impeccably restored rooms. The collection of paintings was so immense and magnificent, and the walls were so crowded with them that I was a little stunned when I eventually exited. Stupefied, I elected to recover at the Café Tulipanen, with rustic tables set among majestic trees near the castle complex, where I had my very first taste of a delicious smørrebrød. Before I left, I made sure to visit the brewery and bought a few bottles of their brew. One should, after all, always support local businesses.

Gavnø done, I recrossed the pretty little stone bridge and left for Copenhagen.

I had chosen a hotel just a stone's throw from Rådhuspladsen, the City Hall square on Hans Christian Andersens Boulevard. Entering Copenhagen, I had the Tivoli Gardens on my right and made a sharp right from Hammerichsgade onto the main boulevard. My little well-appointed room was classy, but cost me an eye-watering four-times the price of my rustic, palatial apartment in Einbeck. This was home for four nights as I explored the city and ventured into Roskilde, Helsingør and Hillerød. The Hotel Alexandra also had a courtyard I could park my car in – accessed via a tiny, narrow passage which set off all the sensors in every corner of the car each time I drove through it. It was a most stressful way to start and end a day when the car's sensors wailed hysterically at me every time I used this passage. Invariably, I breathed a sigh of relief when the car survived unscathed when I successfully manoeuvred through it.

I lost no time after checking-in and immediately headed out, keen to orientate myself with the city and find the Hotel Royal which was Anne's home for nine weeks before she moved to her apartment at 158 Amaliegade. Hotel Royal was built between 1796 and 1798 and occupied the corner of Ved Stranden and Fortunstræde, its main entrance fronting the Slotsholmens Kanal. In

1833, the four-storey building comprised of a basement and three floors, but in 1886 was raised by one additional floor. Many famous people stayed at the prestigious Hotel Royal between 1798 and 1876, among them Danish novelist Bernhard Severin Ingemann, German philosopher Friedrich Schleiermacher, Hans Christian Andersen and the lady who broke Andersen's heart when she turned down his marriage proposal in 1830, Riborg Voigt. Today, the building is home to the Nordic Council of Ministers, an official body facilitating Nordic cooperation between Denmark, Finland, Iceland, Norway and Sweden.

From her window, Anne had a view of Christiansborg Palace, newly constructed following the devastating fire of 1794 in which the first palace was entirely consumed. The Neoclassicism style of the second Christiansborg Palace, built between 1806 and 1828, was inspired by ancient Greek and Roman architecture. However, the structure was short-lived and stood for only fifty-six years before it was destroyed by yet another conflagration in October 1884. The Christiansborg which stands today was built between 1906 and 1928.

As I stood in front of the building that was the Hotel Royal, I willed it to speak to me – to tell me the secrets held within its walls of the time when Anne was there. It stared back, silent and impassive. Undeterred, I set off for the colourful and picturesque canal of Nyhavn to stop by the home of Hans Christian Andersen before strolling along Amaliegade. Andersen used to live in number 20, where he wrote *The Tinderbox*, *Little Claus and Big Claus* and *The Princess and the Pea*.

It was a hot day in Copenhagen when I arrived. The temperature hovered above thirty degrees Celsius, and I was not quite expecting Scandinavia to be quite so warm. The walk to Ved Stranden and then towards Amalienborg Slotsplads was unmercifully scorching, not helped by my detour via Nyhavn and Kongens Nytorv. When I arrived at Amaliegade, the sight of the equestrian statue, Rytterstatuen, greeted me, standing sentinel at the convergence of four streets that divided the courtyard of Amalienborg into equal portions. Amaliegade would have been a prestigious address in 1833. All the buildings there exclaim wealth and nobility. I walked up and down the entire length of Amaliegade, looking for number 158, which proved elusive. The last numbered building on the street was 49 and I even explored the street adjoining Amaliegade, just in case I had missed something. It was much later that I learnt that the street had since been renumbered, and 158 Amaliegade is today's number 3. In any case, it was redeveloped in the mid-twentieth century and is now unrecognisable from the building which once stood there.

Dejected that I could not find 158 Amaliegade, and affected by the heat, I walked into a tiny pub near Nyhavn. It was now half past five and though the sun was still high, it was certainly 'beer o'clock'. I had a quick chat to the barman who was delighted that I showed such an interest in Danish brew. He proceeded to give me a tasting of everything he had on tap. We became very good friends, and I sat at the bar by his taps chatting away as I drank my large glass of Fynsk Forår, a smooth, pale, hazy beer redolent of spring and elderflower. It was so deliciously unique I later trooped over to the supermarkets to search for it and purchased four half-litre bottles, which added significant weight to my backpack. However, I bore it stoically for I was in training.

One of Anne's routines while in Copenhagen was walking along the main road which connected Copenhagen to Roskilde at a determinedly fast striding pace, sometimes resulting in blistered feet. *'Thro' the Roskilde Gate to the ½ mile (about 2 or 2 ½ English miles) straight and back thro' the town not direct as I went out. Neat suburb (faubourg[3]) almost all the way to the palace[4] and good (macadamised[5]) road beyond there. Good avenue of limes[6], ash, oak or elm, all the way – nice walk along the roadside'.* She once timed her pace when she walked

---

3. *faubourg* (French): suburb

4. Frederiksberg Palace, near the current Copenhagen Zoo.

5. Macadamise: to construct or finish a road by compacting into a solid mass a layer of small broken stone on a convex well-drained roadbed and using a binder (such as cement or asphalt) for the mass (Merriam-Webster).

6. The English call Linden trees lime trees, though not closely related to trees that produce lime.

from the Roskilde road, near the quarter-mile milestone from Copenhagen to the little village of Glostrup, '*to the 1 ½ milestone and back to the ¼ milestone in 3 10/.. hours. Therefore walked 2 ½ Danish miles = (if 1 Danish mile = only 4 1/8 English miles) about 10 ½ English miles in 3 10/.. hours*'. In a letter to her aunt which she summarised in her diary, she mentioned walking '*7 English miles along the Roskilde road about 3 days a week*'.

This was what I was in training for. I was determined to walk the seven miles on the Roskilde road.

That evening, in an effort to consume carbohydrates in preparation, I sat down to a large plate of black truffle carbonara pasta washed down with a very nice glass of Barolo.

I chose the relative quiet of early Saturday to recreate Anne Lister's seven-mile round trip along Roskilde road. I calculated that I would have to walk from my hotel on the corner of Hans Christian Andersens Boulevard and Studiestræde to Damhussøen lake, and back again to make this distance of seven miles (11.26 kilometres). Next, I had to figure out an optimal pace to match her own. This proved a little tricky. At the time I planned this walk, I had not yet transcribed her journey of 1833 and so I was forced to extrapolate. Angela Steidele wrote that Anne once covered a six-mile walk from Ripponden to Halifax in two hours. Speed is equivalent to distance divided by time. Therefore, a six-mile walk in two hours would equate to a speed of three miles per hour or about five kilometres per hour. This meant that I would have to complete the seven-mile walk within 2.33 hours, or two hours twenty minutes at an average speed of 12.5 minutes per kilometre.

I felt that this did not seem too daunting a task. So, I thought that the terrain from Ripponden to Halifax was perhaps very hilly or punctuated with swampy bogs full of nasty creatures that she had to shoot at or wrestle with. Therefore, I gave myself a target of ten minutes per kilometre to beat. I set off at exactly six forty-two in the morning, the temperature at a balmy seventeen degrees Celsius (sixty-two degrees Fahrenheit) with a humidity of eighty-eight percent, and twenty percent chance of precipitation.

The walk took me through the mainly urbanised neighbourhood along Roskilde road. It being early Saturday morning, the pavement along the drinking venues of Vesterbrogade was littered with the aftermath of Friday night. It was only when I hit Roskildevej proper, at the Søndermarken park when the walk became prettier.

I was determined to walk as fast as I could, sure that whatever pace I set might be insignificant when compared to Anne's. I jaywalked[7] at every traffic light, reasoning that since they did not exist in 1833, Anne would have needed to stop for nothing. I also suspected that I might have an unfair advantage, I was powered

---

7. An illegal activity subject to a 700DKK (€94) fine.

Denmark

by the music from my iPod, which I neutralised by not eating any breakfast. In addition, Anne would have been dressed in keeping with the times: chemise, stays, several petticoats, skirt, long sleeves, waistcoat, perhaps her great coat, or a pelerine[8]. I on the other hand, had the benefit and comfort of breathable and wicking Under Armour active-wear, a pair of Swiss-engineered running shoes coupled with German-designed compression socks and the requisite underpants and sports bra. My entire outfit, shoes included, weighed a mere seven hundred grammes. It is not inconceivable, from the list of clothes she normally wore, that she might have borne a couple of kilogrammes in clothing. If I had had to put on all the clothes she normally wore, I probably would have passed out by the second kilometre.

I completed the walk in about one hour and forty-eight minutes, averaging nine minutes and two seconds per kilometre which translated to a speed of 6.64 kilometres per hour; an equivalent of fourteen minutes thirty-two seconds per mile or 4.13 miles per hour. If I were to pit my speed against that of her pace to Glostrup, I would still have beaten her by nearly one mile an hour. I gave thanks to modern clothing and good music.

---

8. A woman's cape of lace or silk with pointed ends at the centre front, popular in the nineteenth century (Oxford).

Back at my hotel, pleased at my achievement, I had a long shower. Then, I got underway to Roskilde, the ancient capital of Denmark between the eleventh and fifteenth centuries. In October 1833, three weeks after arriving in Copenhagen, Anne and Lady Harriet went on a two-day excursion to Roskilde and Ryegaard. I myself made my way to Roskilde's Domkirke after first spending the late morning at the Viking Ship museum north of the old town.

> *Roskilde, the ancient capital of Denmark, but now a nice neat village-like little town. Nice little inn, 4 Danish miles from Copenhagen. Had stopt half way at 9 37/.. to 10 50/.. to bait the horses. At Roskilde at 11 25/..*
>
> – 10 October 1833

From the inn, where Anne noted disapprovingly, '*Lady Harriet took warm rum and water*', they set off to the nearby Roskilde Domkirke. This impressive cathedral's construction began in 1170 and has been rebuilt and renovated so many times that it is now a superb showcase of eight hundred years' worth of Danish architecture. The royal mausoleum contains the crypts of thirty-seven Danish kings and queens. I was surprised that Anne did not notice the animated medieval clock from the fifteenth century; each hour, Saint George strikes the dragon and it lets out a frightful wail. The poor thing has been beaten mercilessly every hour for the past six hundred years.

> *In the cathedral at 11 55/.. for 1 ¼ hour. Fine old Gothic, very neatly kept, white washed, plafond painted (over the plaster a running pattern) church. Handsome covered pulpit and fine organ and handsome piece of old oak painted and gilded carving over the altar, the Life and Death of Christ. Some very handsome marble sculpted royal tombs and below, the six little coffins of the present king's children. One born before the time, another four hours old, and one about a year old – none but the tombs of royalty and some few of the old noble families here – a new chapel (royal) in the Corinthian Greek style tho' very handsome in itself, not in keeping with the rest of the church. A granite pillar there (said to be from Italy) evidently formed by putting two short ones end and end together – on this column the height of Christian I marked equal to 3 Danish ells[9] and 10 inches and under this Peter the Great of Russia marked about 3 ½ English inches shorter. The church 140 Danish ells long and 41 ditto high.*
>
> *– 10 October 1833*

---

9. 1 Danish ell = 24 ¾ English inches (*Handbook for Travellers in Denmark, Norway, Sweden & Russia*, J. Murray, 1839)

After seeing the church, they left for Ryegaard to visit a friend of Lady Harriet's, the 59-year-old Princess Varvara Alexandrovna Vjazunskaja of St Petersburg, the widow of Niels Rosenkrantz[10], the former Danish Minister of Foreign Affairs. Since her husband's death in 1824, Madame Rosenkrantz lived in the estate, sixteen kilometres north-west of Roskilde, which is now run as Ryegaard og Trudsholm Godser, a hospitality venue.

However, Madame Rosenkrantz did not warm to Anne. They discussed Russia but she did not offer to write Anne letters of introduction. Over a dinner of anchovies, lamb steaks and cold suckling pig, Madame Rosenkrantz mentioned she was going to St Petersburg in May. Lady Harriet commented that Anne was thinking of going too, but the princess made no comment for Anne to call on her in Russia. Nor did she want to shake Anne's hand which made the situation quite unbearable for Anne who was staying the night at her estate with Lady Harriet.

She shook hands with difficulty last night. Like a goose I offered my hand this morning which she positively declined and, on my hoping to see her often this winter she said as little as possible.

What is the matter with the woman? I fancied it might be reserve and shyness as she is so good and

---

10. Dansk Biografisk Leksikon

> poor, nothing but a pension from the king. But I think now it must be pride? She is a stately dame and Lady Harriet says is cold about shaking hands.
>
> – 11 October 1833

Anne, feeling frustrated and out of place at dinner, muttered into her diary in code, '*I cannot make out if she likes me, but fancy not. Dullish evening – to tell the truth, very stupid evening*'.

The next day they left for Ledreborg Slot, a castle built between 1740 and 1745 by the Count of Holstein-Ledreborg. Anne could not help herself from moseying around.

> *The regular man who shews the place not there as the summer is over. A country man shewed us to an unmeaning sort of summer house, wood-built moss house in the wood. Then to the little mount where the Holsteins are buried (nine counts lie buried there – a small obelisk erected to the memory by the late Comte[11]) and then unable to find the Runic antiquities I had expected, just walked thro' the nice garden in front of the house and off at 2 37/.. Saw the vegetable preserving house by accident – a long, low, narrow room about 3 feet sunk into the ground, with servants' rooms above. A double flue or stove*

---

11. *comte* (French): count

> *pipe goes thro' the middle holes, like pigeon-holes, in the brickwork between the top and bottom flue, the height about as high as half the height of the room. The stove like a covered up little lime kiln or oven at one end, and the flues opening out at the other. The other end of the room full of potatoes – cones of carrots at the sides of the room and in the recesses of the window to be blocked up in winter – cauliflowers, parsley, etc. etc. All with good roots set close packed in sand – the carrots to be covered with sand or sandy mould.*
>
> – 11 October 1833

They set off home via Roskilde and Anne arrived back at the Hotel Royal, *'glad to be back'*. She had noted disapprovingly several times in her diary the number of occasions Lady Harriet indulged in rum. Anne's mother was an alcoholic and it obviously weighed on her. Even the next morning, when she sat at her desk to write the events of 11 October 1833, she felt compelled to note, *'Lady Harriet very good, but too chilly and rum drinking'*. Little did Anne suspect the strain Lady Harriet was under during her marriage to Jasper de Hagemann.

I returned to Copenhagen after my day-trip to Roskilde. I reckoned the fast-paced walk in the morning and the packed day of sightseeing was deserving of a nice, smooth beer. I moseyed into a pub just after five o'clock. Then, after an early dinner, I carted myself to bed because another big day awaited me.

I slept with the window open, and the morning breeze woke me on that cloudy, mild Sunday in July 2019. Soon I was heading to the Vor Frue Kirke, Copenhagen's cathedral. Vor Frue Kirke, which was built on the highest point in the heart of the city at Nørregade, was one of the first landmarks Anne visited in Copenhagen. She too visited on a Sunday, with the de Hagemanns on 22 September 1833. The unfortunate church had suffered a slew of misfortunes throughout the centuries. Its first version was destroyed in a fire in 1314. There were further fires resulting from lightning strikes in 1573 and 1585. Rebuilt, it was then completely destroyed in the Great Copenhagen conflagration of 1728. Not a century later, the dastardly English, led by General Lord Cathcart and Admiral James Gambier, sent a shell targeted at its spire and almost completely destroyed it during the 1807 Battle of Copenhagen. Rebuilt according to Christian Frederik Hansen's plans, the new Vor Frue Kirke was consecrated on Pentecost day in 1829. The church was initially installed with Bertel Thorvaldsen's *Christ and Twelve Apostles* in plaster, but later replaced with the finished marble sculptures, starting with *Christ* in 1833 and completed in 1848 with the installations of *Andrew* and *Judas Thaddaeus*.

In 1839, when Anne returned to Copenhagen with Ann Walker, she visited the church again.

> *The Twelve Apostles by Thorvaldsen very fine. The St John and St Matthew said to be the best. He cleverly made them too big for niches. The Christ, the chef d'œuvre[12], en niche, and too much darkened and spoiled, over the altar. Plain, handsome building in good Greek taste (Doric) – but too white.*
>
> *– 16 July 1839*

Pity the luckless Danes; firstly the English blew up their church, then travellers complained that it was either too dark or too white. The Dane I met was quick to point out that before the English blew up their beloved church, the spire stood 120 metres tall, and could be seen halfway to Roskilde. The current tower, my new acquaintance moaned, is only sixty metres tall. I confided I was Malaysian-Australian and whispered that my motherland, Malaysia, was once colonised by the imperialist English. We shared a knowing nod. I tactfully withheld the fact that my long-suffering other, poor Chris, is English born and bred.

From Vor Frue Kirke, I made my way to the Rundetårn, an observatory built in memory of Denmark's famous astronomer, Tycho Brahe, who died in 1601. Apparently, the British also tried to destroy this astronomical tower

---

12. *chef d'œuvre* (French): masterpiece

in 1807 by launching more than a hundred Congreve rockets in its direction. Miraculously, it survived the bombardment and thankfully so. Built between 1637 and 1642, it is Europe's oldest observatory. The unique tower is thirty-six metres tall, ascended by a spiral corridor high and wide enough for men mounted on horses. In 1716, Czar Peter the Great of Russia rode his horse to the top, while his wife was rumoured to have followed behind in a light carriage or cart. Unfortunately, Anne could not ascend the tower because it *'could not be seen without an order – for people went up and committed suicide by throwing themselves down. A woman did it only a few days ago'*.

Next for me was Christiansborg Slot. I bought my ticket and entered the vast complex. Christiansborg Slot was the palace that Anne visited with Lady Harriet, Sophie Ferral and her sister, Countess Blücher.

> *The large new palace opposite (almost) my window. The pictures not to be seen today. An hour (with several people there) in the museum of old Scandinavian curiosities – spears, hatchets, rings, etc. found in tumuli*[13]*. Then an hour walking over the palace. A round room, very prettily panelled in differently stained wood, and the top (quite flat) made to look domed by being done in large flutings (like an*

---

13. tumulus, tumuli (plural): ancient burial mound

escallop shell). First peeped into the large unfinished room, will be like the great assembly room in York, only a balcony all along above the fine Corinthian columns – handsome chapel. Then peeped into the handsome cour de premiere instance[14] (from which no appeal, and where the king presides in State[15] the first Thursday in every March – not used as yet. The president of the court begs to go on longer in the present place. The old palace of Fredericksborg[16] burnt down 7 years ago – the workmen had left some chips at the top of the palace and something or other that inflamed them.

– 26 September 1833

It took me three full hours to tour the palace, its stables, kitchen and the ruins of the fortress of Bishop Absalon under the complex. Its rooms were splendid, the Alexander Hall especially so, being beautifully appointed with the restored Thorvaldsen marble frieze, *Alexander the Great enters Babylon*. Despite the sensory overload after the palace, I felt I had to visit the museum of Bertel

---

14. *cour de première instance* (French): trial court
15. Council of State – all acts of legislation and other decisions in the Council of State must be sanctioned by the king.
16. Here, Anne meant the Christiansborg on the island of Slotsholmen in Copenhagen opposite the Hotel Royal. Because Frederik VI was king at the time, she called Christiansborg Fredericksborg, which is not to be confused with Frederiksberg on the Roskilde road.

Denmark

Thorvaldsen. This great man who had been gifted with hands from which celestial sculptures came into being. Thorvaldsen's museum is situated on Slotsholmen, the very island on which the palace is located. Thorvaldsen himself is buried in the inner courtyard of this museum which is dedicated to him. Over his lifetime, he made over ninety free-standing sculptures, nearly three hundred bas-reliefs and more than 150 busts, in addition to large quantities of drawings, sketches and maquettes. When she toured his studio with Ann Walker in 1839, Anne herself described Thorvaldsen *'is to Copenhagen what Praxiteles was to Athens'*. On seeing his creations for myself, I must admit that I wholeheartedly agree.

Having skipped breakfast and with no time for lunch, I munched on an apple as I made my way to Rosenborg Slot, Christian IV's seventeenth-century summerhouse with gabled facades, turrets and moat, fronted by a pristine and well-maintained garden. It was here that Anne *'sauntered about'* and admired the *'fine bronze statue of a lion having just sprung upon a horse prostrate, and in the act of tearing his side'*. The Rosenborg Slot now houses the Treasury, home to the dazzling crown jewels of the Danish monarchy. While the crown jewels were certainly dazzling, it was the arsenal of weaponry that really impressed me, a collection of ceremonial and functional weapons dating back to the seventeenth century.

The next day, I made a side-trip from Anne's 1833 journey to follow in the footsteps of her 1839 excursions with Ann Walker to the ancient castle of Kronborg in Helsingør and to Frederiksborg Slot in Hillerød, the royal residence of Christian IV. I drove to Helsingør first, wanting to beat the crowds and having studied Shakespeare at school, I was especially looking forward to this day. It was forty-seven kilometres north of Copenhagen, or about twenty-nine miles. I had learnt that a couple of good horses should take between eight and twelve hours to convey a carriage fifty miles, when not driven by a German postilion. In reality, Anne and Ann travelled to Helsingør from Frederiksborg. If they had travelled directly from Copenhagen, it would have taken them nearly a whole day to get there. My journey took less than an hour – forty-six minutes to be exact.

Located on a strategically important site commanding a view across the Øresund, the stretch of water between Denmark and Sweden, the royal castle of Kronborg at Helsingør is of immense symbolic value to the Danish people. It played a key role in the history of northern Europe between the sixteenth and eighteenth centuries. In the 1420s, Eric of Pomerania built the first castle, the Krogen, on this unique site. Then, a century later in 1574, work began on the construction of this outstanding Renaissance castle. Its defences were reinforced in the late seventeenth century according to the canons of the period's military architecture. It has remained intact to the present day. It is world-renowned as Elsinore, the setting of Shakespeare's *Hamlet*.

I explored every exhibition room carefully, delved into the dark and eerie casemates where Holger the Dane still sits sleeping and climbed the very same tower-steps ascended by Anne Lister and Ann Walker to enjoy the view from the top.

> *Ann and I, with laquais de place*[17] *walked to the castle of Kronborg in 10 minutes – 151 good steps, winding staircase to the platform roof from which we had fine view of the Sound and Swedish coast and island of Wien*[18].
>
> – 19 July 1839

Then Anne sought out '*the room in which Caroline Matilda was confined. Shewn 50 steps high into the suite over it. Could not see the veritable because now occupied by the governor and his wife – disappointed*'.

Christian VII's banished queen, who had a penchant for wearing male riding attire with scarlet coats and buckskin breeches, was imprisoned in Kronborg in 1772. Accused of having a love affair with her husband's physician, Johann Friedrich Struensee, Caroline Matilda was incarcerated in Kronborg for several months while

---

17. *laquais de place* (French): cicerone, guide who understands and explains antiquities, places of interest etc.
18. Island of Ven, south of Helsingør.

she awaited her fate. Her two children were taken from her. When the affair came to light, Struensee was arrested, sentenced to death and decapitated, then dismembered. Caroline Matilda was later exiled to Germany where she died at the age of twenty-three in Celle.

I do not remember visiting Caroline Matilda's suite. However, I do remember the Great Ballroom which was sixty-four metres long and used to host sumptuous banquets. A typical banquet could consist of up to twenty-four heavily spiced dishes, including crayfish in aspic, massive joints of venison, oysters with costly lemons, pâté of swan, hare and lobster. There were also rooms exhibiting seven of the extant fifteen Kronborg tapestries. The original number of forty-three tapestries, depicting portraits of a hundred Danish kings were commissioned by Frederik II around 1580.

From Kronborg, I made haste to Frederiksborg Slot.

The Dutch Renaissance Frederiksborg Castle is beautifully situated on three small islets of the Castle Lake in Hillerød. The oldest part of the castle dates from Frederik II's time, though most of the present structure was built by his son, Christian IV in the early decades of the seventeenth century. The castle is the largest Renaissance complex in the Nordic region. I had never before seen anything so splendid and fine and the castle chapel was unequivocally stunning.

Saw the chapel first – the plan of the cathedral at Copenhagen might have been taken from it, except that the covered or vaulted ceiling here is much gilt, and the whole chapel instead of being plain white is all carving, in-laying and gilding – but the same sort of portico runs all round the chapel at mid-height, and the royal chapel in Christiansborg at Copenhagen is also on thus a plan. For the altar of this latter, Thorvaldsen's Christ was originally intended, but is of course better where it is. Thorvaldsen then proposed a Virgin and Child for the altarpiece in the Royal Chapel but Prince Christian's observation that we had nothing to do with this sort of thing in our religion, put an end to the thing and now there is to be something I forget what.

– 19 July 1839

The altarpiece is one made of gold, silver and ebony commissioned in 1606 from the Hamburg goldsmith, Jacob Mores. Above it is the Compenius organ, built in 1610 and installed in 1617 by Esaias Compenius of Eisleben, Germany. The modern tourist is fortunate to gaze upon these wonders, because the chapel survived unscathed the 1859 fire which destroyed large parts of Frederiksborg Slot.

The exhibition rooms of the castle are rich with antique furniture, royal portraits, coat of arms and its crowning glory, the Rittersaal.

> *Ritter saal – Knight's Hall, large handsome room with rich oak-carved painted and gilt panelled plafond – large black marble chimney piece at one end. Some king of Sweden tore off and took away all its massive silver ornaments. The chimney grooved or channelled from bottom to top, the channel beginning at about 8 inches wide at the bottom on a length with the hearth increasing in breadth to perhaps 16 or 18 inches wide, and perhaps so much as 5 or 6 inches deep all the length. The chimney wide enough to sit in at the bottom and narrowing to a flue perhaps 18 inches square at the top – never smokes.*
>
> *– 19 July 1839*

Anne might have been captivated by the fireplace at the end of the hall, but the Rittersaal, having been reconstructed as faithfully as possible from the room before the fire of 1859, is a magnificent space with a lavish, jaw-dropping gilt and carved ceiling and walls decorated with tapestries and royal portraits.

I spent the rest of the afternoon wandering in the centuries-old Baroque gardens, an extensive landscape of carefully tended trees and gorgeous blooms. Finally,

I returned to Copenhagen late in the afternoon, and that night, my sleep was pervaded with dreams of castles.

Uncharacteristically, while Anne was in Copenhagen between 18 September and 30 November 1833, she did not explore the city and its surrounds as much as I thought she would have. She did venture to Charlottenlund and Eremitageslottet, the Hermitage hunting lodge in Lyngby which is sixteen kilometres north of Copenhagen. However, she spent her time mainly with her friends, chatting over meals and attending operas. She *'made a grand mistake in supposing the music of Robert le Diable by Rossini! By Meyerberg – fine but laboured. Got over my blunder as well as perhaps such a blunder could be got over. What in the world do I know of operas?'* She also spent time walking along the Roskilde road and the quay of Langelinie. Having enjoyed her travels through Germany, she decided to turn her attention to improving her German. '*I am so pleased with Germany, I think of travelling about there the next spring – but not knowing German is terrible, so I have made up my mind to have a master*'.

She was thinking of visiting the Leipzig fair, and potentially Berlin and Dresden in April 1834, but was woeful of her progress in the study of the language, exacerbated by the fact that she kept falling asleep over her work, which she blamed on the sun. Nevertheless, during the autumn of 1833, she persisted.

On 28 September, she was, '*at German till 3 20/.. wrote out what I had translated and the lesson of yesterday and translated by myself and slumbered a little now and then*'. Two days later, she '*wrote out fourth lesson translation and that of this morning (slumbered a little over the latter – the sun hot in my room) till 3*'. On 2 October, '*from 2 ¾ to 5 10/.. (had a little nap the sun so hot) at German – translated into English the little letter I had written in German this morning*'. She was still struggling on 6 October, recording her studies took place '*from 12 ¾ to 4, at German (but asleep half the time)*'. The following day, she was much the same, noting, '*German and slumbering (no sun today – yet very sleepy). From 8 ½ to 11 at German writing out translation (2 pages) for tomorrow and every now and then asleep – how very sleepy and lethargic I have been of late!*' Only on 2 November was there any suggestion of progress, '*from 11 ¼ to 12 ½ at German – I improve tho' slowly*'.

She wrote and received plenty of letters to and from England and sent an entire barrel of Norwegian anchovies to Miss Tate in a show of gratitude for her hospitality while Anne was in London. The letters from Mariana affected Anne most. Mariana still hoped her husband, Charles, would die. However, in spite of the cholera-like illness from which he suffered, he would not expire. Charles's brother, William Lawton, the runner up in Mariana's hopes for financial security, died before his time. Now she was considering a Willoughby Crewe. It really did seem as though she would only take Anne as a last resort. No matter their affectionate letters and obvious closeness, there always appeared to be a final barrier before them. Anne, despite her self-assurances that she no longer wanted to set up home with Mariana anyway, was deeply affected.

> *Thinking of Mariana last night in bed, even to tears. More satisfied this morning. Let her take Willoughby Crewe. She will never again suit me? Why be like the dog in the manger about her? Heaven has withheld what I for long so fondly wished and I am satisfied it was for the best.*
>
> – 20 September 1833

Anne also 'thought much of Miss Walker' and agonised whether to write again to Mrs Sutherland. Undecided, she turned her attention to her social life in Copenhagen, and the highlight of her stay was an audience with Queen Marie Sophie Frederikke of Denmark, arranged by Peter Browne, the British chargé d'affaires, who, though a very nice man and well-liked, 'had dirty nails'. Dressed in a black satin gown, with her black blonde pelerine[19], Anne was introduced to court.

> *Unluckily took the chief maid for the queen because of her broad red riband order and star. Got over it well enough and did not care so much as I might have done. About 10 minutes audience of the queen ætatis[20] about 65, a nice neat little figure looking very well but sadly too much rouged. Very gracious and agreeable. Then to Princess Caroline, the king's daughter that was burnt; her throat and lower part of her face still bearing strong traces of the fire. About 5 minutes with her. Not au fait[21] at audiences like the queen – not much to say for herself but very civil.*
>
> – 23 October 1833

She also met '*Princess Christian (Caroline Amalie) very handsome, very dignified*' with whom she discussed the Vor Frue Kirke and Thorvaldsen's statues of the Twelve Apostles. That evening, she wrote in her diary in crypt hand, '*I wonder what they all thought of me. It was a great gaucherie[22] to mistake the Dame de Honneur this morning for the queen but perhaps I shall get over it*'. Whatever Anne may have thought of her *faux pas*, the queen liked

---

19. Shawl of black Chantilly lace.
20. *ætatis* (Latin): at the age of
21. *au fait* (French): up to date and well-acquainted with something
22. *gaucherie* (French): embarrassment, awkwardness

her enough and invited Anne to her birthday ball. In preparation, Anne had Eugénie make her a white satin dress, *'impossible to go to a birthday in black – merely throw it off for the night,'* from material she purchased from Hertfort's, along with some *blonde*[23].

Finally, the much-anticipated event arrived.

> *Mr and Mrs Browne called for me in coupé at 7 ½ – crowded of course. One of my oiseaux*[24] *de Paradis came down in the carriage. Mrs Browne arranged it on arriving at the queen's palace. Countess Blücher and Miss Ferral had been there some time. About 8 the cercle*[25]*. Might be about 50 ladies in front and as many behind, and perhaps half as many more. The queen, and Princess Christian Caroline Amalie, then Caroline Princess Royale and then her young sister, Wilhelmina followed round the circle. Mrs Browne stood between Mrs Stuart Courtenay and myself to present us to the king as the queen begin with the lady half [of] the aire*[26]*. The king began with the gentlemen half and each went the whole round.*

---

23. Chantilly lace were called *blonde* for their original pale colour.
24. *oiseaux* (French): birds
25. *cercle* (French): circle
26. *aire* (French): area

Then to the ballroom all following the royal family. Dancing at 12, then 30 ladies and 30 gentlemen drew lots for each other and all the rest of us went to the Grand Marshall's table (in the king's palace, up and down dirty, narrow stairs and along long low passages) at which his deputy Mr Crow presided. The ex-Dresden minister's wife on his right and I on his left, a perpetually handed round supper but nothing looking particularly good to eat; but took some quince and some blanc mangu[27] – a glass of goodish Rudesheimer, and a glass of tolerable champagne to drink the queen's and Princess Charlotte's birthdays. The president gave the health – drink in silence. A third birthday today, but not mentioned.

We then went back (only 5 ladies besides Mrs Browne and myself, all the rest had gone home) to the salon, saw the royal party (excluding king and queen) again and there got to our carriages as soon as we could. Set down Mr and Mrs Browne and home at 3 35/.. Everybody very civil to me – very well amused – but now that I have seen the thing once, will not trouble the Marshall's table again. Not fond of second tables even in the houses of kings. The party said to be usually small – no diamonds but

---

27. *Mousse de fromage blanc à la mangue* – a white cheese mousse with mango.

those worn by the royal family. Princess Christian the finest woman in the room and Miss Ferral the prettiest best dressed girl. No magnificence of dress but everything assez bien[28].

The palace moderately handsome. All the princesses polite to me conversationally particularly Princess Christian and Princess Wilhelmina. She asked me if I had been much in the grande monde[29]*. I answered 'no, not very much'. Princess Christian admired my head dress. I said I had had grand peur*[30] *about it. It had come down and Mrs Browne had arranged it. One of the queen's maids of honour observed my magnificent blonde and said, 'was it not from Paris?' 'Yes, but I had bought it here. Was in black and had nothing white with me. Could get everything good but stockings'.*

I shall know better what to say by and by. How they know everything here! I generally on coming away remember some gaucherie, but I don't care. I shall learn in time.

– 30 October 1833

---

28. *assez bien* (French): pretty good, good enough
29. *grande monde* (French): big world
30. *grand peur* (French): great fear

Anne had attended the queen's birthday ball with Sophie Ferral and her sister, Countess Blücher. Countess Blücher, née Emily Sophy Mary O'Ferral, was born in St Croix and several years older than Sophie. In 1826, at the age of twenty-four, she married Gustav Carl Frederik von Blücher, the son of Conrad Daniel von Blücher, in Copenhagen. Conrad Daniel von Blücher was a highly respected, well regarded diplomat among the Danish royalty. He studied in Copenhagen at the Landkadettenakademie military academy and through his military achievements was appointed in 1808 as president of Altona, which was under the administration of the Danish monarchy between 1640 and 1864. He was raised to the rank of count in 1817 as a result of his contribution to the city and his heroic efforts against the French during the occupation of Hamburg. The Blüchers, though not the richest of families, were as *haut ton* as Anne would have liked any of her inner circle to be. Anne found Countess Blücher fascinating, and noted that she '*reminded me of Lady Eastnor, that gentle interesting manner*'.

Missing from the night's festivities was Lady Harriet. There was a strange dynamic in the friendship between Anne and Lady Harriet. Lady Harriet obviously liked spending time with Anne, and they called on each other often, but she was reluctant to introduce Anne into society. Even with Jasper de Hagemann's close ties to the royal family, Anne's invitation to meet the queen came not from them, but the chargé d'affaires, Peter Browne. Perhaps there was a petty jealousy, as Countess Blücher alluded to Anne once. Browne too had confided in Anne that the de Hagemanns were not well liked in society, '*Mr de Hagemann brusques*[31] *the court because he has no rank there, and the king is not all a man to be bullied. Mr de Hagemann is in fact nobody, and gives himself too many airs*'. Countess Blücher shared this sentiment, '*Countess Blücher and I talked of the de Hagemanns. How foolish they are about the court and how he gives himself airs and is therefore not liked and she [Lady Harriet] made unhappy*'.

Browne had even gone so far as to say he would have called on Anne earlier, were it not for the fact that he thought she was staying at the de Hagemann's. '*He evidently does not like them*,' Anne confided in her diary.

De Hagemann's brutish manner extended to his home life as well. As Lady Harriet became closer to Anne, she confided in Anne of his fiery temper, '*and her being frightened out of her wits, and therefore not managing him well*'. Lady Harriet, herself the daughter of a British governor-general, had never been presented at court, a fact de Hagemann blamed on the Danes for their dislike of the English. He thought, '*if his wife had been a German, she would have been differently treated, but the English not liked*'. Anne '*wondered [if] they would*

---

31. *brusque* (French): abrupt, rude

go to the court. Poor fellow, he little thinks it is he himself that is not liked?' Anne concluded, *'what geese they are'*. Perhaps it was de Hagemann's behaviour which drove Lady Harriet to the bottle.

As autumn settled in, Anne considered moving out of the Hotel Royal and started the search for an apartment. Through her new friends in the inner circle of the *dame d'honneurs*[32] to the royal family, she found No. 158 Amaliegade. De Hagemann helped in the inspection and rent was settled for fifty species[33] – about £11[34] – with curtains and carpet, and an equipped kitchen all included. Lady Harriet stepped forward and assisted in finding a cook for Anne. She received the key to her new apartment on 16 November and a week later, on the twenty-third, finally completed the move.

In mid-November, Anne woke up to a gloomy, rainy Tuesday morning. Waiting for her was a letter dated 10 November from her sister, Marian, and Dr Kenny. Perhaps the weather forewarned of the ominous contents.

---

32. *dame d'honneur* (French): maid or lady of honour – junior attendant attending to a female member of the royal family
33. A concurrent currency to the Danish rigsbankdaler.
34. Between 1813 (after the Danish financial crisis) and 1838 (when the species achieved parity with the rigsbankdaler), the Danish rigsbank skilling was valued at 96 skilling to 1/2 a species. 96 skillings equalled 1 rigsbankdaler. £1 was equal to about 9 rigsbankdalers. Therefore 50 species = 100 rigsbankdaler = £11. Adjusted for inflation to 2020's purchasing power, Anne's apartment would cost about £1,318 today.

Denmark

Her aunt, said Dr Kenny,

...is at present in an exceedingly precarious state of health. Both legs have been more or less oedematous for some time past, but one in particular became very much so within the last few weeks, and a small ulcer which lately formed upon it, has assumed a most unhealthy aspect: indeed within the last few days, it has increased rapidly in extent by a gangrenous state of the surrounding skin and cellular membrane. At present it has a defined margin, but the slough has not yet wholly separated. In the enfeebled state in which your aunt's general health is found at the present day, it is impossible to say whether the gangrene may at any time extend rapidly beyond the present limits, and lead to a fatal termination. With so much constitutional disturbance the pulse is as might be expected constantly above 100. If I were to hazard an opinion which might tend to influence your plans, that is whether you should or should not return to this country at present, it would be this – Gangrene possibly may upon any day extend rapidly and destroy life long before you could possibly arrive in this country. On the other hand, the gangrene having at present set limits to itself, the sphacelated part may slough away, leaving an ulcer, which need

not necessarily destroy life, tho' I do not anticipate under any circumstances its evincing a disposition to heal soon, if ever.

– 19 November 1833

Marian's letter though not as alarming, provided little comfort to Anne.

I know you cannot come home, for my aunt has no idea of any danger, and I fear it might be a great shock to her. She remarked yesterday that she should be better or worse in a few months – I asked why? She thought she had not stamina to bear so much suffering long.

I afterwards when I could without creating suspicion, said, if she would like to have you here, were I her, I would send for you, she said no, you could do her no good.

I had before said something of the sort, but she thought it nonsense tho' were she in danger she should wish to see you – that I trust you will so manage matters, that without alarming her, you can come over in the spring or early in the summer tho' I still persuade myself she will struggle on till autumn but I am concerned to say the swelling of her limbs does not in the least abate... the worse leg is as much swelled in a mound as the better one is at right. Dr Kenny fears the skin bursting... my aunt is very cheerful when her suffering is not very great.

– 19 November 1833

Anne wanted to dismiss them both as '*old alarmists*' and did not know what to make of the letter, but its contents continued to haunt her. She wrote back to Marian the next day, '*tho' my aunt had told me all about the breaking of the skin and the sore, persuaded myself, and tried to persuade her, it might be good for her and prolong her life – accustomed to think Dr Kenny an alarmist, but wish to hear from him and Marian again, and also from Mr Sunderland*', the latter being another medical man whom Anne held in higher regard than Dr Kenny. Amidst the chaos of moving into her apartment on Amaliegade, her aunt's condition continued to weigh on her mind. At one point, several days after she had moved in, Anne, '*on looking in the glass, struck with the black hollow round my eyes*'.

On 28 November, Anne received yet another letter from Marian and her aunt, '*perhaps the last my poor aunt will write*'. Her aunt was then so frail, it took her three attempts to complete her one letter. The first section, dated Saturday, 16 November explained that she had trouble holding her pen. The second, dated Tuesday, 19 November explained that she was in so much pain the previous days she could not finish her letter. She described to Anne the sore on her ankle, which *'has amassed to nearly the size of half a crown, discharges a good deal of thin waterish looking matter and looks dark green around the edge, and is very painful'*, and the other sore *'on the leg that discharges a little'*. Aunt Anne had *'so much pain and inconvenience from the scaley flakes breaking, that I am obliged to have plasters put upon them'*. In the section dated Wednesday, 20 November, she tried to assure Anne that she *'had a tolerably good night, and feel better this morning. Tho' the pain is certainly not much abated, the discharge from the wound rather less waterish'*. She continued to reassure Anne that she had every possible comfort and that Marian was doing all she could *'to alleviate any sufferings'*, that her servant, Cordingley, was very attentive and that Dr Kenny and Mr Sunderland visited her often. Aunt Anne was also very pleased that Anne was enjoying her time in Copenhagen.

The letter was finished by Marian, who wrote that Aunt Anne was not aware of the danger she was actually in, and that even she did not dare tell her aunt how precarious her life was. She beseeched Anne once again to return especially when Mr Sunderland alarmed her, saying that the gangrene would be fatal. She said the wound looked no worse and that *'Dr Kenny does not seem to be under any immediate apprehension'*. Although Marian was anxious as the wound was gradually enlarging, she assured Anne that their aunt was composed and cheerful, *'but I trust she may have the comfort of seeing you, and you of being with her'*.

Anne stood, *'fixed over my letter'* her mind racing. Finally, she was spurred into action, *'I will be off immediately'*.

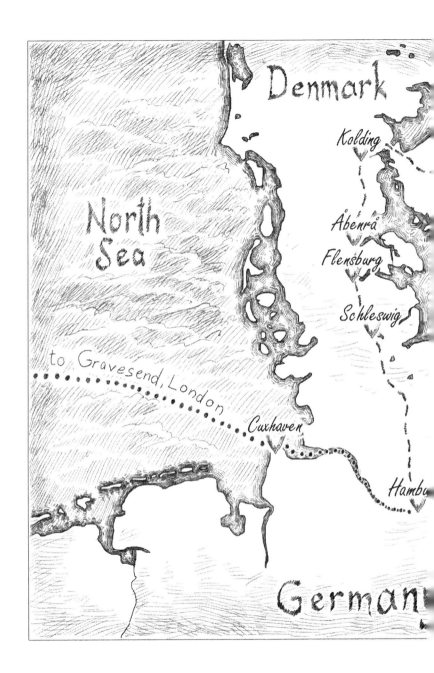

Anne Lister's route home from Copenhagen in 1833

Chapter Eight

The Rush Home

There was a flurry of activity leading to Anne's departure from Copenhagen on 30 November 1833. Her friends rallied around her, except for Mr de Hagemann who urged her to stay, saying that she could do no good by going and that her aunt would die before her arrival. Worse, he was more mindful of the optics of her departure than of Aunt Anne's health. De Hagemann *'put it upon the expense and my health, and how odd people would think it, and how it would be talked of'*.

Lady Harriet however was supportive and thought Anne was right to return. One of Anne's new friends, Count Vargas-Bedemar, a charismatic personality who helped manage Prince Christian's mineral collection, offered to arrange for a courier.

There were two distinct roles for a courier in the nineteenth century. One was appointed for the despatch of letters, mainly diplomatic or military missives, which had to be delivered confidentially and more quickly than the ordinary mail coach could manage. The other was a quality servant, an expensive luxury superior to a valet de place, who was employed by the wealthy. These couriers were multilingual, speaking the language of the country with ease and able to manage the complexities of foreign exchange. They also assisted in procuring horses at each post-relay and in securing accommodation at a fair price.

They considered appointing one of the servants from the Hotel Royal as her courier for a cost of fifty species, but it was Peter Browne who suggested that Anne abandon that idea and that she travel instead with Lord Hillsborough[1], who possessed a diplomatic courier's passport for the urgent despatch of letters. This would mean that they would be given priority to the horses at each post-relay. It was anticipated that Anne '*could be in England in a fortnight – across the Belts[2] in three days*'.

---

1. Arthur Wills Blundell Sandys Trumbull Windsor Hill, Earl of Hillsborough and fourth Marquess of Downshire (1812-1868). In 1833, he was serving with the Royal South Down Regiment of Militia, first as an ensign, then promoted in September to the rank of lieutenant-colonel.
2. The Storebælt and Lillebælt are straits between the Danish islands of Sjælland and Fyn, and Fyn and the Jutland Peninsula, which led into the Duchies of Schleswig and Holstein and to Germany.

The Rush Home

Two days after receiving the letter from home, Anne, her servants and Lord Hillsborough were ready to depart. Just before leaving, Anne took aside the not-ugly-but-stupid-and-odd, Miss Ferral, '*and gave her one of my little Rodgers 15/. mother-of-pearl penknives from Sheffield, saying 'see if this cuts away your love before my return*". Miss Ferral dumbfoundedly stared at the sharp implement, uncertain what she could possibly do with it and could only murmur '*that is very nice of you*'. Anne '*staid not to hear more*' and left, confidently thinking '*I really think she has some regard for me*'.

At last, they departed from Copenhagen in the afternoon, '*off at 3 55/.. with regret to leave behind so much real and flattering kindness, yet deeply anxious to be home in time to see my poor aunt alive*'.

They were past Roskilde in four hours and it being '*too dark to see anything*', Anne '*slept most of the way*'. Soon they passed Ringsted, thirty-one kilometres south-west of Roskilde, and halfway to Korsør, where Anne was to cross the Storebælt, the first of the two Belts.

I myself had picked up Anne's trail again in Korsør. In July 2019, I did not know for sure which route she took and both Choma and Steidele's books did not state exactly where she crossed the Belts. However, I had a hunch she would have crossed the Storebælt from Korsør into Nyborg and crossed the Lillebælt between Middelfart and Snoghøj. Travellers had been sailing the fourteen nautical miles between the ports of Korsør and Nyborg even before Eric of Pomerania in 1396. As it turned out, my hunch was correct. Nearly a year later during the first corona pandemic lockdown of 2020, I sat in my study, transcribing her diary. I could feel her words, formed under stress and anxiety, reveal themselves under my fingers as I typed faster and faster, my shoulders taut with the strain of suspense and concentration.

In Korsør, I visited the Korsør Town & Crossing Museum. I was the only one there and I spoke to the elderly volunteer who manned the little place. He was eager to share his knowledge, and I, a willing listener. The first official passenger ferries began to operate in 1883. Anne would have crossed either by merchant ship or the packet ship. I surmised that, with her carriage, it was conceivable she would have used the packet ship which commenced its service in 1828. Much later, I was delighted to find a bill of passage for the *Mercurius* among Anne's papers in the West Yorkshire Archives Service. Following an intense crash course in learning Danish, and aided by my intermediate German, further investigation in the Danish archives allowed me to learn that Anne did travel across the Storebælt on Denmark's first ever steam packet ship, which had plied the fourteen nautical miles between Korsør and Nyborg since 1828.

The *Mercurius*, built in England, was Denmark's first Post and Telegraph Service steam packet ship. She was 70-feet 3-inches long and 11-feet 11-inches wide between the paddle wheel arches. In the stern was a spacious cabin that was described as *'simple but comfortable and neat'*. Two water closets completed the ensemble. The *Mercurius* burnt 255 kilogrammes of coal per hour, generating twenty-eight nominal horsepower[3], or thirty-two metric horsepower, which fuelled a speed of 7.5 knots enabling the vessel to cross the Storebælt in an hour and fifty minutes[4].

Steam technology was so new to the Danish that they had to appoint an English engineer, Edward Allingham, at a princely salary of £8 per month, plus board and lodging of £3 and four shillings. The steamer was not without its problems, and initially the two-cylinder side-lever engine caused considerable trouble. Anne herself experienced this, noting that *'about halfway the engine was stopped for about half hour – something broke. For a little while thought the accident could not be repaired and we must make for another port'*, and she also mentioned the English engineer, Allingham, *'Mr Allan, or some such name, the engineer'*. Mr Allingham remained as engineer for the *Mercurius* until 1838 when he was let go for economic reasons.

---

[3]. Nominal horsepower (nhp) is an early nineteenth-century rule of thumb used to estimate the power of steam engines. Brown, David K (1990), *Before the Ironclad*, Conway, p. 188

[4]. Bell, Poul – *H/S Mercurius, Storebæltsfartens første Dampskib, Jahrbuch Handels- og Søfartsmuseet pa Kronborg*, 1974, s. 7-15

Almost everything that Anne Lister did was steeped in historical significance. The *Frederik den Sjette,* on which she travelled from Travemünde to Copenhagen was the first ever steamship built in Denmark, and now she travelled on the first ever steam packet ship utilised by the Danish Post and Telegraph Service.

At the Korsør Town & Crossing Museum, I learnt that the Storebælt sometimes iced over and travellers had to drag their boats over the ice. Many were equipped with massive saws to cut through the ice. They could not use dogs and sleds as they did in Greenland because there would be pockets of water amongst the ice. Anne was fortunate she crossed in early December and it was not iced over, but even then, Allingham had said that '*it goes 5 days a week but will only go about a dozen times more this season*'. After the season closed, the crossing could only be attempted with ice-boats, which Allingham described as '*the strongest boats he ever saw in his life*'.

I felt I had to see these boats for myself and travelled to the Isbådsmuseet, a tiny museum with a handful of ice boats, near to where the Storebælt bridge spanned the water. The ice boats were extremely solid dinghies, each with a high central keel and an iron membrane shod under the keel that could function as a sledge runner. The boats were pulled over ice when the surface was frozen, or sailed on water when the ice broke. One trip could take between three to six hours, sometimes longer if the occupants had to walk roughly twenty-six kilometres across the Storebælt in bad weather.

Rising behind the Isbådsmuseet was a narrow path to a ridge which afforded a sweeping view of the expansive Storebælt. I scrambled up its sandy path and stood there in silence. It was surprisingly cold and windy on that ridge. I observed the water, watched it peak and froth, and how the waves broke against the rocky shore. It was July, but the surface was rough and the overcast sky made the water look unforgivingly cold. Anne crossed in December, and I shuddered to think what the conditions were truly like.

> *Off at 11 5/.. Rough water. Good deal of wind but not against us. Such a spray splashed over, I soon went into the cabin with Lord Hillsborough and another gentleman who had been remarkably civil to me at the inn. Lay down immediately – slept about 10 minutes or quarter hour then began to be very sick (this driving my gentlemen away) and continued so the whole way.*
>
> – 1 December 1833

The *Mercurius* landed in Nyborg at twenty minutes past two in the afternoon, three hours and fifteen minutes since her departure from Korsør. I crossed the Storebælt by driving across the Storebæltsbroen, the bridge which was inaugurated in 1998 at a cost of 21.4 billion Danish kroners. My crossing, in a car with a 335-horsepower V6 engine, took me just under ten minutes.

Anne arrived into Nyborg, green but empty. Together, she and her companions sought dinner at a nearby inn. She then realised that the civil gentleman, upon whom she nearly vomited, was '*Comte Ahrnsfeldt*', a gentleman she had once met at the Blücher's and who owned the entire island of Langeland. This person was actually Christian Johan Frederik Ahlefeldt, Count of Ahlefeldt-Laurvig, a descendant of an ancient noble family. Between 1832 and 1856 he was owner of the tremendously magnificent Tranekær castle on Langeland island, south of Nyborg, and well regarded in the area. The proprietor of the inn, a wine merchant, laid out the very best for them.

> *The master of the house is a wine merchant and certainly has good wine for Comte Ahrnsfeldt. Gave us a bottle of excellent white Burgundy and 3 bottles most excellent red. Ditto a Château Margeaux, which Lord Hillsborough carried off better than the comte whose French was certainly more stammering at last than at first. He was most civil, begged Lord Hillsborough to make a party with Comte de Blücher and some other friends and go and take a hunt in Langland. We had bouillon[5] in China cups, and boiled fish (haddocks?) cut in pieces about 1 ½ inches*

---

5. *bouillon* (French): broth

The Rush Home

long, and excellent beef steaks, and almonds and raisins for dessert.

– 1 December 1833

Refuelled, the group departed Nyborg at quarter to five and travelled to Odense, '*in 2 25/.. hours, 4 Danish miles about 17 English miles, proof of the goodness of the roads. Finding by carriage lamp light (the town not lighted) Odense seems a largeish good town*'. They did not stop in Odense, hurrying through the night to Middelfart to cross the Lillebælt.

I, on the other hand, was not constrained by time. I felt romantically compelled to stay two nights in Odense, the birthplace of Hans Christian Andersen. I had delusions of sauntering peacefully through the homes and museum of Hans Christian Andersen with the fairy tales I was brought up on, vivid in my mind.

This was not to be the case.

On arriving at the museum, I found that Denmark's entire population of children were amassed there. It being nearly four o'clock, they had obviously been robbed of their afternoon naps and were the crankiest lot of children I had ever encountered. Never having been compelled to have children, the sight was quite terrifying. One poor child was screaming and banging her head against a glass exhibition case. Her lungs were so powerful, her parents must have endowed upon her the genes of the *Fylgjur*, a wailing Nordic banshee someone sees when one is about to die.

I rushed through the museum in ten minutes and visited the other sites spread across the Odense Old Town in another forty-five. These included Hans Christian Andersen's birthplace, his childhood home and the Museum of Cultural History. My limited education from the museum was that Andersen was born on 2 April 1805, died 4 August 1875, his mother died in 1833, and he had intense relationships with both men and women.

Traumatised and shell-shocked by unruly children, I sought refuge in the only place where I knew I would find relative peace, a brewery. Nursing a cold lager at Bryggereit Flakhaven, I vowed never again to follow my romantic inclinations.

The next day, I steered clear of anything related to Hans Christian Andersen. Instead, I went for a short hike on the Enebærodde promontory, a reserve with very nice views. There was complete silence but for the chirping of birds and the waves breaking against the idyllic beach. Then, I made my way slowly towards Egeskov Slot by way of Klintebjerg. The castle of Egeskov was originally built in 1554 but it has been in the possession of the Ahlefeldt-Laurvig-Bille family since 1784. Throughout the centuries, Egeskov was primarily an agricultural operation. Then in 1960, tired of it looking like a farm, Countess Noni and

Count Gregers set out to create one of Denmark's most ambitious garden projects and turned the surrounding lands into a remarkable parkland.

On her own journey, Anne had made her way to Middelfart.

> *At Middlefart at 12 50/.. at night – had been raining heavily for some time for the last 2 hours. Lord Hillsborough and Thomas much wet – the former wanted to go on and cross the Belt immediately. Thomas, who is not very hard, begged to stay to dry his clothes. Told Lord Hillsborough he would find it cold work across the Belt and persuaded him to stop. It blew hard and rained hard.*
>
> *– 2 December 1833*

They stayed at the inn in Middelfart, drying their clothes and dozing until quarter past six in the morning. They drove along a nice road for twenty minutes to the small harbour then spent ten minutes loading the carriage on board a large open flat-bottomed sailing boat. They crossed the Lillebælt in ten minutes. At Snoghøj, they found that the Post had no horses.

> *But on seeing Lord Hillsborough's courier's passport, the postmaster quite another man. Took four horses for us from a waggon standing by (obliged to get us forward) and off from Snoghoi, merely the post house*

and a good-looking inn, at 7 ¾. The Belt here is merely like a fine bending river, the opposite coast of Fyen or Funen rather wooded and undulating and pretty. The little town of Middlefart, with its whitewashed church tower, pretty enough from Snoghoi.

– 2 December 1833

The church that Anne described is St Nicholas church. It is also referred to as Middelfart church since there has never been more than one church in the town. Around 1200, the current brick structure probably replaced an older church made from unhewn stone. The Renaissance-style pulpit dates back to 1596 and the pews are the oldest parts from the sixteenth century. When I visited there were whalebones which date back to 1603 over the door to the tower. The bones were from a large whale and consisted of two under jaws, two fragments of the upper jaw bones and an unspecified bone.

After visiting the church, I strolled along the old harbour, Gammelhavn, then drove to Kolding, which I had believed was Anne's next stop. I was rewarded when my transcription of Anne's diary revealed, '*Kolding a tolerable little town with large unfinished modern-looking château, and old ruined castle tower close to it. Nice enough little inn at the Poste. Honest people – charged only ten Hamburg schillings = 10 pennies English for the cheese and ham and bread (thin slices of cheese or meat laid on buttered bread) and a small glass of rum Lord Hillsborough had*'.

The Rush Home

However, Anne did concede, *'with a little more wood the Belt and environs of Kolding would be charming'*. Today, Kolding is more than merely tolerable and the old, ruined castle and surrounding grounds that Anne saw are charming. Koldinghus was founded in 1268 by Christoffer I to protect Denmark's border from the Duchy of Schleswig. The castle was reduced to a smoking rubble in a catastrophic fire in 1808 and lay in ruins until 1890 when locals took the initiative to rebuild it. It is now a museum worthy of a visit if in the area.

The travelling party continued south towards Hamburg's Altona gate, with Anne disapprovingly noting that the young Lord Hillsborough *'constantly takes a small glass of rum like coachmen and such-like'*.

They were through Flensburg at one thirty in the morning, then their rumble[6] fell apart in a small town two hours north of Schleswig. For a quick fix, they *'tied it up with cords – Lord Hillsborough sat astride of the travelling bags on the boot and lastly stood on the rumble step behind as we entered Schleswig and Thomas mounted the off-wheeler'*[7]. At *'Schleswig, finely situated on an inlet of the Belt, good, large town'*, they spent an hour *'greasing*

---

6. An exterior seat at the rear of the carriage mainly for footmen. The passenger would be exposed to the elements.

7. The horse on the right-hand side of the coachmen is referred to as 'off horse'. A wheeler is the strongest horse hitched closest to the carriage, that can help in slowing the vehicle when required. The off-wheeler is the horse closest to the carriage on the right of the coachman. E. Cobham Brewer 1810-1897. *Dictionary of Phrase and Fable.* 1898

wheels and putting travelling bags behind to make Lord Hillsborough a tolerable seat on the boot'. From here, they encountered again the terrible roads renowned in the territories of Schleswig and Holstein, where Anne noted the *'road bad enough to Schleswig, still worse from there – deep sand, with deep ruts full of water. In places, the road mended with heather'*. They stopped to bait the horses, and Lord Hillsborough offered Anne a taste of his corn brandy, *'I tasted it – took not more than a teaspoonful. Seemed like fire in me, tho' did not taste strong in my mouth. Quite white, like water'*.

Soon they were on the direct route which ran from Kiel to Hamburg in the Duchy of Holstein – an artery maintained well by the duke in order to monopolise and divert trade traffic from Lübeck. *'Really very good – a fine new macadamised chaussée*[8]*. Never go to Copenhagen by Lübeck again. Tho' be it remembered there are no custom house potherations*[9] *at Lübeck, and an infinity of them at Kiel'*.

Their pace picked up, and eight hours later they arrived at the Altona Gate. They had travelled through the night, in stormy weather, *'the rain again at times very heavy, came pouring down in large and small drops – terribly stormy, windy, rainy night'*. Outside, Thomas

---

8. *chaussée* (French): road
9. potheration: fuss, turmoil, trouble

The Rush Home

and Lord Hillsborough were wet through. It was half past five in the morning, and the gate was closed.

The Altona Gate marked the entry into Hamburg, accessed by the hilly suburb of Hamburger Berg. The suburb was demolished during the Napoleonic wars in order to have a clear field of fire in front of Hamburg. However, it was quickly repopulated and restored following the French withdrawal in 1814. In 1833, Hamburger Berg was re-named St Pauli. Between 1820 and 1837, Hamburg authorities started to dismantle its fortifications and convert them into parks. The old city gates which had stood for centuries were facing demolition, but the Altona Gate remained to demarcate the city limits. It was also a revenue generator; travellers entering as dusk fell and before dawn were levied with a fee. This gate fee was eventually abolished at the end of 1860 and the Altona Gate demolished. A reminder of the historic gate was erected in the form of the cast-iron Nobistor posts. One, which survived World War II, stands in the dodgy district of St Pauli on the Reeperbahn.

It was this obscure post that I set out to find when I arrived in Altona at about five thirty in the afternoon on Thursday, 18 July 2019. My visits to Hamburg had never once included a trip to St Pauli and the streets of the Reeperbahn, the area now populated with shady bars, adult-themed entertainment establishments and all the unpalatable trappings that came with them. My hotel, though respectable, had rooms decorated in shockingly gaudy colours. My main purpose in Altona was to find the Nobistor post and then a beer in a relatively decent pub. I walked the Reeperbahn in search of the Nobistor. First, I went too far west, looking for the post on a street called Nobistor which, ironically, is not where it is located. I finally found it just a few steps east of the Beatles Platz, in front of an establishment called the Paradise Point of Sex – a mega-brothel with a hundred rooms with services starting at about €50.

Finding the post, though an exciting undertaking, was a little anticlimactic. After all, it was just a black, iron-cast post inscribed with some Latin words. A little plaque set into the pavement contained a commemoration about which no-one today really cares very much. I self-consciously took a photo and then headed across the street in search of a beer, where the surroundings were slightly less dodgy.

Faced with the shut Altona Gate, and feeling cold and wet, Lord Hillsborough came to the party's rescue. He produced his courier's passport and despatches, and the gate was opened for them. In less than forty-five minutes, they pulled up in front of Mr Hillert's Hotel zur Alten Stadt London. Anne waited at the hotel while Lord Hillsborough rushed to find out if they had missed the steamer to England, '*Yes! Off at 3 in spite of wind and weather*'. Having missed the steamer by just several hours, Anne considered travelling back to England another way. The Consul-General, Mr Henry Canning, whom Lord Hillsborough introduced to Anne, '*half tried to persuade me to go by Rotterdam – should be in time for the packet of Wednesday and then be certain of being in London on Thursday, but owned that if the weather was not very bad, I might be in London on Monday or at farthest Tuesday by the Columbine from here at six on Saturday morning*'. The helpful Mr Canning sent Charles Delaval, the steam packet agent, to further advise Anne.

> *He said the journey to Rotterdam took 90 hours and with my heavy carriage might take now from 120 to 130 hours. Roads very bad, often no regular road at all – made of heather and sand from Bremen till getting into Holland. Had I set off yesterday morning could not have been in time for the Saturday packet from Rotterdam but if off tomorrow, might be in time for that. But he thought me right to keep to the determination of going by the Columbine. Had I arrived by 12 on Tuesday night it would have been an hour too late to embark the carriage even embarking it at 11 would have been dangerous, it was such a stormy night – this satisfied me.*
>
> – 5 December 1833

Anne now had no choice but to wait for the Columbine which was scheduled to sail in the early hours of Saturday,

7 December. She occupied her time by writing letters to thank her friends in Copenhagen for the kindness and support they had afforded her during her stay, and when she made the decision to rush home, *'whatever may be the faults of the English, they are not ungrateful'*, as Miss Tate of 21 Grosvenor Place, London would have found out, very likely by now sitting in a sea of anchovies.

For an inexplicable reason, Anne Lister's friendship with Miss Tate was a source of great fascination to me. Miss Tate must have been exceptionally nice to Anne to merit an entire barrel of Norwegian delicacy sent all the way from Copenhagen.

Anne referred to her only as Miss Tate and described her as *'an elderly maiden lady, very plain, neither much mannerism nor haut ton, but very musical'*. From piecing together a few scant diary entries, I learnt that Miss Tate lived at 21 Grosvenor Place when in London and also had *'her place Langdown, near Southampton'*. Based on that, I started my sleuthing and as it turned out, Miss Mary Tate of Langdown House was truly a kind soul, renowned for her charity work. She was about fifty-six years old when she first met Anne in London. She owned not just the property on Grosvenor Place and in Langdown, but also Burleigh Hall in Loughborough, Leicestershire and a large house on Mitcham's Cricket Green in Surrey. As an only child to George and Bridget

Tate, Mary Tate inherited his properties upon his death in 1822[10].

Being female in the nineteenth century had its downside. Some sources have even obliterated her from history, stating that George Tate had died without issue. However, heiress Miss Tate lived in her various properties until the age of seventy-three when she died at Burleigh Hall in March 1849. Her cause of death was recorded as, *'ossification of arteries, paralysis'*. As she never married, Queen Victoria granted the surname Tate to her cousin, Louisa Pinfold in July 1849, per George Tate's last will and testament.

Upon receiving her inheritance in 1822, Miss Tate set up a home for the mentally ill utilising her large property in Mitcham. Several years later, she demolished the building in order to purpose-build almshouses on the site. These provided enough accommodation to twelve women in need, be they *'old servants or decayed tradeswomen*[11]*'*. Her legacy of generosity and kindness remains to this day. The Mary Tate Almshouses on 14 Cricket Green, Mitcham, still function as a refuge for women in need. The benevolent Miss Tate is buried at the Mitcham Parish Church, St Peter and St Paul, just a three-minute walk from her almshouses.

---

10. Burke, John – A Genealogical and Heraldic History of The Commoners of Great Britain and Ireland, Volume II, 1835
11. Croydon Almshouse and Relief in Need Charities

Miss Tate must have been not just generous, but extremely modest too for it seemed that she had not revealed her extensive charity work to Anne in 1833, who would have undoubtedly recorded it in her diary. However, it appeared that Anne was a good judge of character and sensed the compassionate soul that resided within Miss Tate.

Through Lady Harriet, Anne obtained a barrel of anchovies for the price of one Danish daler and four marks, equal to about four English shillings – about £24 today. She had it sent to Lady Stuart for her butler to forward to Miss Tate, with a note *'merely to say I had great pleasure in sending her a barrel of Norwegian anchovies that I only hoped she would like. I thanked Miss Tate for her so kind inquiries after me and my plans. Should not plan my future route till March, the time of my departure. Often thought of Miss Tate and her good advice'*.

Norwegian anchovies are actually not anchovies at all. They are sprats of the *Clupea sprattus* family, also called brislings. The fish was first classified[12] in 1758 by Carl Linnaeus, a Swedish naturalist whose work was also known to Anne Lister. The Norwegian anchovy measures anywhere between seven and sixteen centimetres long with shiny, silvery scales and has a life span of less than

---

12. Linnaeus, Carl – A General System of Nature through the Three Grand Kingdoms, Volume 1, 1806

five years. It spawns between January and August, but more intensively in the months of May and June.

In the nineteenth century, the premium sprats were first cured in a strong salt brine in large wooden barrels with a capacity of 140 litres, holding about ninety-five kilogrammes of fish. After the salting process, they were drained and then rolled in a spice-curing mixture which was comprised of sugar, salt, cloves, nutmeg, black pepper, Spanish hops and allspice. Then the sprats were packed in layers in a sweetened brine in half-barrels. Some recipes included saltpetre, bay leaves, cinnamon or ginger. The barrels were then rolled about or inverted regularly. The curing process was complete after two weeks. The sprat fillets were then repacked along with the filtered curing brine in smaller 3.5-litre barrels, producing the Norwegian-style anchovy so sought after and enjoyed in Europe. In 1831, imports of Norwegian anchovies from Christiania (Oslo) to England had increased from 7,390 barrels in 1829 to 9,413[13], but its main markets were chiefly in Sweden and Germany.

In the earlier decades of the 1800s, before advances in canning techniques, the spiced anchovies would have rarely kept for more than three or four months, after which they were considered overripe. So, once Miss

---

13. Selection of Reports and Papers of the House of Commons: Finance, p. 555, Volume 27, 1836

Tate received her gift she would have had about two good months to eat them all.

Anne also wrote to Madame de Bourke in Paris and diplomatically *'said Miss Ferral was a most agreeable, sensible, useful companion de voyage, never making difficulties'*.

After the letter-writing marathon, she turned her attention to her stopped-up bowels and *'took two spoonsful of Epsom salts[14]'*. The next morning, she was rewarded with *'two good but watery motions, one at five and the other on getting up'*.

Her letters written and sent, and her bowels loosened, Anne boarded the Columbine at nine in the evening on Friday.

> *Walked on deck till 11 ½ p.m. and then crept into my cot. Did not undress, nor shall I, during the voyage. Only 4 berths in the cabin at the stern and nobody but Eugénie and myself. The wife of a captain of a large Russian vessel with a nurse and two children and one gentleman and perhaps one or two steerage passengers besides Thomas and that is all. Fair all today for a wonder. High wind (during the day and now) and right against our getting out of the river – F48° at 11 ½ p.m.*
>
> – 6 December 1833

---

14. Magnesium sulphate, a chemical compound known as Epsom salt was used widely for many ailments, including constipation.

The Rush Home

Anne woke up aboard the Columbine on Saturday morning, '*on deck at 8 ¾ and were then twelve miles English from Hamburg*'. The ship had weighed anchor as she slept, and was now steaming north-west on the Elbe towards the North Sea.

On my own journey, I left Altona early on Friday morning. My next destination was Cuxhaven, the last town in my quest to follow Anne's footsteps through the Continent and Denmark. I could have taken the Autobahn 7 and then picked up the 73 into Cuxhaven, but because Anne sailed on the Elbe, I felt I had to do the same. So, I headed north out of Altona and drove on a lesser autobahn and then followed quaint country roads flanked by crops, to cross the Elbe. The ferry service, Elbfähre, operates every thirty minutes between Glückstadt and Wischhafen. As the ferry pulled away from the port and made its way towards the middle of the Elbe, I could just make out Glückstadt behind me. The city was founded in 1617 on the marshlands along the Elbe by the Duke of Holstein, King Christian IV of Denmark. He had levees and fortifications built as well as a ducal residence. Its name translates to English literally as 'Luck City' or 'Fortune City'. I exited my car and stood at the bow, the breeze cool and fresh, and with an occasional spray of water when the wind picked up.

Anne's navigation of the Elbe was not quite so idyllic and by ten she was sickish. The weather turned and the drizzle, which confined Anne to her cot, had become an *'incessant rain'*. She finally got up *'and find we have been for about two hours, since 2 ½ p.m., at anchor in Cuxhaven harbour, the wind being too strong for us to venture out to sea'*.

Anne ended up stranded in Cuxhaven for a total of five days. On Saturday night, they experienced *'heavy rain and high wind all night'*, and *'to prevent our rolling about in the night, the captain had run us up within the wooden breakwater. The wind was so high we broke from our moorings and at midnight ran foul of the pier and broke our bowsprit*[15]*'*. When Anne emerged from her cabin, members of the crew were busy making a new one with an old schooner-bowsprit the captain had bought on shore in Cuxhaven. Even after repairs, the unrelenting storm, hail and high winds kept them from their onward journey. Anne spent the lazy Sunday killing time, *'incurred a cross thro' my drawers thinking of Mariana (but not affectionately)'*. Mariana, and her dramas of Willoughby Crewe, had become a figure to encourage the release of Anne's sexual frustrations. Anne considered her now, not as a prospective wife, but as a raunchy, sexy mistress, and, as such, she *'incurred a cross thinking of Mariana. Oddly, merely as a mistress'*.

---

15. A spar extending forward from a ship's bow, to which the forestays are fastened. Bowsprits significantly enhance the performance of the sail and allow for easier manoeuvres and sail handling.

The Rush Home

In the afternoon, she went on shore with Thomas and the captain.

Walked about the North Holland-like, little gable-ended town, hid behind a sort of breast-work so that not much of the town is seen from the water. A good looking inn with good public room and billiard table in it for the sea-captains and people near to the water. A little beyond, the round brick tower lighthouse which stands on a sort of dyke or embankment sometimes overflowed and ingeniously covered over with straw-matting such as our men at home make for door mats. By this means the mud is held together and one can walk over it comfortably. Never saw this sort of thing done anywhere else. From the inn clean walking along a dyke, along a sort of deep long dry dock or canal with a row of houses along the opposite dyke, and after a little distance a street at and along the feet of the dyke I walked on.

At the end of this dyke and dry canal went down into the nice little paved town. Walked half round the moated brick house-like castle or garrison, with a few guns pointed over the breast-work towards the mouth off the river about 30 miles from here. Neat little town enough – gardens from the houses down to a sort of canal divided by a nice lime-shaded walk from the castle moat. This it was reminded me of North Holland but there were no pretty bridges.

– 8 December 1833

The same lighthouse which Anne saw greeted me as I parked my car at the Cuxhaven harbour. The Hamburger Leuchtturm of Cuxhaven was built between 1802 and 1804 by the Free and Hanseatic City of Hamburg, to which Cuxhaven then belonged. The lighthouse is one of the landmarks of the city and was in operation until 2001. The tower cost 102,000 marks at that time and was put into operation on 15 November 1805. In this almost four-foot-thick, four-storey and 23-metre high lighthouse (with a fire height of twenty-four metres) is a total of 104 steps to the tower fire in the eighteen-cornered lantern. The lantern, under a copper-covered hood has a diameter of five metres and consists of three superimposed rows of windows made of flat mirror glass. The original tower fire consisted of seven so-called Argand reflector lamps. These were special oil lamps with a round burner, also called an Argand burner after its inventor, Aimé Argand. The lamps were initially operated with rapeseed oil. To begin with, the beacon beamed so far that it could be seen quite well at sea even from about six kilometres away.

From the lighthouse, I walked to the historic pier that Anne's ship '*ran foul of*' and stepped onto the Alte Liebe (Old Love). The Alte Liebe is the former pier in the port of Cuxhaven, which today is used as a viewing platform. It is located on the upstream boundary of the Cuxhaven harbour to the mouth of the Lower Elbe. The Alte Liebe was first built in 1733 by the sinking of three disused ships at this location. The ships were surrounded with stakes and the space filled with stones and brush. The goal was to fortify the harbour from damage by storm surges and to protect the lighthouse which then marked the port entrance. Later, the Alte Liebe served as a jetty.

The name Alte Liebe is said to derive from the foremost of the three sunken ships called Liebe (Love). According to another tale, the name of the ship was Olivia. However, it was only called Oliv by the locals, which corresponded phonetically to the Low German word for 'Old Love' (Ol 'Leev). From the pier, I walked into the old town and chanced upon the Schloss Ritzebüttel, the former castle residence of the Hamburg officials when Ritzebüttel was part of Hamburg. The castle, which dates back to the fourteenth century, is one of the oldest surviving secular buildings of the North German Brick Gothic in the region.

While stranded in Cuxhaven harbour, Anne spent some of her time reading or picking up on obscure bits of information, discovering that, *'to soften ivory, steep it in a decoction of sage, made by boiling sage in strong vinegar; to cure a corn, roast a clove of garlic on a live coal or in hot ashes and bind it on the corn on going to bed; the Columbine can carry 75 tonnes of coal exclusive of cargo; Rotterdam and Hamburg mails are conveyed by the steam company's boats for £13,000 a year; passage to America 30 guineas*[16] *and there to India £100; once a fortnight every voyage of the Columbine to Hamburg and back costs about £300. Crew = 21 at £50 a week, wages exclusive of the captain's £160 per annum. Carpenter has 28/. a week and men 21/. a week; albumen (white of egg) remarkable for the preparations of making leather supple and a solution of it in water used therefore by leather dressers'.*

On Wednesday evening, the weather was still no better.

> *Wind tonight and rough water – our vessel heaved about so much before the tide raised her quite off the ground, that at 9 I was really sick, and got rid of all my tea and bread and butter.*
>
> – 11 December 1833

After incurring yet another 'cross' whilst thinking of Mariana, she got up on Thursday morning to find that the ship had sailed and Cuxhaven was already far behind. The weather was tolerable, and there was not

---

16. The guinea was minted from gold and got its name from the Guinea coast which was fabled for its gold. From 1717 until 1816, a guinea equalled £1.1s. (21 shillings). After which, the guinea was a colloquial term and was considered a gentleman's currency. Tradesmen, such as carpenters were paid in pounds, but a gentleman, such as an artist or barrister, would have been paid in guineas.

much wind, although what wind there was blew against them.

> *At 1 ½ rain sent me to my cabin, and this and the rough water made me sick immediately. Threw myself on the hair covered bench at the foot of the cots and sick and retching almost incessantly for the next eleven hours.*
>
> *Tho' somehow about ten at night crawled in the dark into the water closet and had a tolerable motion, so far a good effect of my sickness.*
>
> *The wind was, soon after getting out of the river, in our favour. Towards evening the vessel rolled so tremendously nothing not very fast could keep its place – my table and stool were turned upside down to slide about that way. My candle was set in a basin jammed in the table bottom, the candlestick danced about so in the basin, I could scarce help laughing. Cooler on the bench than in the cot, and more convenient for being sick, so there I lay in my cloak and fur travelling cap with my travelling bag for a pillow.*
>
> – 12 December 1833

The following day, she recorded:

> *Rough night – wind, and rain and snow. The Jolliffe*

and Tourist[17] *no longer in sight. Nothing on my stomach but frequent retching. Sea cross and rough as ever, but wind in our favour – rain or hail perpetually beating against my sky-light. Lay on my bench, 2 or 3 times in the course of the day looking at my watch, and paying for this exertion and indulgence by an extra fit of retching.*

– 13 December 1833

Forty-four hours after sailing from the Cuxhaven harbour, the Columbine steamed beyond the Nore lights, a series of small wooden vessels which guided ships into the Thames from the North Sea. They must have all breathed a sigh of relief when the fine crescent lights along the water's edge of Gravesend were spotted. Thomas and Eugénie had also suffered motion sickness throughout the journey but they were fated to stay yet another night on the ship. It was too dark to dock, and they would not have been able to unload the carriage until Monday at any rate.

Anne and her servants disembarked on Sunday at an ungodly hour of three in the morning and headed immediately to the Ship Tavern at Water Lane, leaving her carriage on the boat. The Ship Tavern was '*a dirty looking place*' but '*anything better than onboard*' the Columbine. She '*remade (threw off) the bed of soft*

---

17. The William Jolliffe and Tourist were two other steamships that were stranded in Cuxhaven harbour during the storms.

feather, and the sheets which had been slept in. Made all as comfortable as I could. Put a towel over my uncased pillow, and my dressing gown to serve as top sheet about my face, and threw myself in bed in my great coat at 4 ¾ a.m.'. After a good five hours of sleep, she got up and had *'a thorough scrub with soap... then had my hair washed, my head needing it after its so long heating in my fur cap'*. Despite the inn's inferior cleanliness, Anne was *'glad to come to the Ship Tavern, after 48 hours sickness – yet whether from anxiety or not, have not once felt fatigued, tho' five nights from Copenhagen to Hamburg without taking my clothes off, and 10 nights from Hamburg here'*.

Now clean, Anne sat down to write to both Mariana and her aunt. Anne was keen to travel via Leamington on her way home to Shibden to see Mariana. To Mariana she wrote, *'have a bed for me, if you can; as the night I spend on the road, I would rather spend with you,'* and to her aunt, *'you may expect me certainly on Thursday evening, by 6 or 7 I hope... my dear aunt, believe me very anxiously impatient to see you'*.

After this entry, dated 15 December 1833, Anne's diary was blank for the next four pages and she resumed writing on Saturday, 21 December 1833. Her diary on 21 December already focused on home routines. She spoke to Charles Howarth about the upper buttery floor. Her aunt was a great deal better than it was possible to expect from the very alarming accounts she had received; she had breakfast with her father and Marian and then became annoyed with Marian and made her cry.

Anne Lister was home.

Afterword

Eadem mutata resurgo
Although changed, I arise the same

Epitaph on the tombstone of Jacob Bernoulli,
Swiss mathematician (1655-1705)

Standing on the Alte Liebe pier, being buffeted by the wind, seemed a fitting end for my journey in Anne Lister's footsteps. That seemed like the moment my life changed, as though it was an invisible yet tangible line which separated my life before I learnt of this remarkable and fascinating woman, and the life after.

On the surface, I am the same person, but in some inexplicable way, I have changed too. I travelled home slowly, returning to Bremen yet again, to face my personal demons. This time, the skies were bluer, the sun brighter, and the air more rejuvenating. I took a few more days to digest Anne's journey, and my own, as I explored Osnabrück and Münster on my way home to Bonn.

Somehow, during my travels, the things I saw came to life and had more historical significance when viewed through Anne's words. Following in Anne's footsteps in July 2019 has put me on a quest to travel to as many places she had travelled to. Seen through her eyes, a weather-beaten memorial of black basalt suddenly revealed an exciting tale from centuries past. A forgotten craggy ruin was now at the forefront, an insignificant building now noteworthy, even remarkable. Travel is enriched when accompanied by the spirit of an adventuress like Anne Lister.

When I drove into the driveway, Chris was already waiting by the garage door. I flicked the switch which opened the boot, then stepped out and with a flourish, gestured at the beers I had accumulated throughout my journey. There was a happy laugh, followed by arms encircling me warmly.

I too, was home.

Anne Lister's 1833 journey was not her last. If anything, it had only served to whet her appetite for travel in Europe. By 14 June 1834, she was once again standing on the pier of Calais. This time with Ann Walker, her life partner, standing next to her. Their remarkable life together was one rich with adventure and discovery.

Acknowledgements

I started transcribing Anne Lister's travel journals and diaries in April 2020. I did so with the encouragement of Janneke van der Weijden, an experienced volunteer transcriber working with the Anne Lister Diary Transcription Project, itself spearheaded by the West Yorkshire Archive Service. At the time, I was interested in Anne's 1827 journey through France, Switzerland and Italy, as there was not much literature available on her travels with Maria Barlow. Muriel Green's compendium of Anne Lister's letters, *Miss Lister of Shibden Hall, Halifax: Selected Letters, 1800-1840* provided me with some information but I desired more. For me, there can never be enough information on Anne Lister.

Anne's handwriting is notoriously difficult for beginners to read. After a shaky start, I began to familiarise myself with her style. Janneke was particularly supportive and proofread my early transcriptions. So did another volunteer transcriber, Dorjana Širola. Dorjana, who ran a fine-toothed comb through my work, helped me understand the nuances of Anne's confounding abbreviations and explained some of the old English words which are incomprehensible to a non-native English speaker. I am forever grateful to Janneke and Dorjana for taking the time to help me gain my transcriber credentials. The 1827 transcription led to the 1833 journey, then the 1829, 1830, 1834 adventures and it kept going. After transcribing Anne's complete 1833 journey in 2020, I set out to explore various towns in France and Luxembourg and several places in Germany, which I had missed, that Anne had visited. I also returned to several locations I had visited during my July 2019 road trip, just to see the landmarks through Anne's eyes yet again. Invariably, they are more meaningful and awe-inspiring when equipped with Anne's words.

In the course of writing this book, I transcribed more than six hundred pages of Anne's diaries and travel journals which, while providing me with a good understanding of Anne and her travels, is just the tip of the iceberg.

The ambition of writing this book would not have been achieved without some help along the way. To this end, I thank Amanda Pryce for her Anne Lister Timeline, which assisted me with understanding Anne's earlier

Acknowledgements

years. Special mention goes to Marlene Oliveira, Shantel Smith, Amanda Pryce, Steph Gallaway, Lívia Labate and Jude Dobson who recently published the article, '*Where is Anne Lister?*' which revealed information on the Lister infant who died in 1806. I am grateful too to the ladies behind Packed with Potential and Diane Halford, co-founder of 'In Search of Ann Walker', who researched how Anne Lister's body had returned from Georgia to England after her death in 1840.

Thank you, Cornelia Krsak, who sent me some maps of the German Confederation from her school textbooks, and Rikke Dahl Nielsen for sharing her research on Anne's apartment on Amaliegade.

I also want to thank and acknowledge the support from the Lister Nerds. They are the minds behind Packed with Potential, the true nerds against whom my passion and interest for Anne Lister pales. Lívia, Marlene, Chloe, Jenna, Jess, Kathryn, Shantel #TeamMariana, Ylva, Steph, Jude, Succotash, Alex, again Amanda, and especially, the very truly French Pauline Marchadié who helped me with the more toe-curling French transcriptions. You are indeed '*French enough*'.

Thanks also to the army of Anne Lister Codebreakers who helped decipher words which confounded me. What a collaborative community we Codebreakers are.

I am grateful to Karen Ip, historian and director of Croydon Almshouse Charities, who shared her research of Mary Tate and to my relief, verified my own. I was delighted to discover there is another person in this world who is as fascinated with Mary Tate as I am.

Many thanks, editor extraordinaire, Paul Roberts. Your advice and guidance have been invaluable.

Of course, the red squirrels in my garden should be acknowledged. They amused and kept me company as I worked – Little Squeek, Twit, Vader, Littlefoot and Teufelchen. My gratitude to them has already been repaid in an abundance of walnuts and hazelnuts. However, if not for the regular distraction of their cute antics, I would have certainly finished this book sooner.

Lastly, let me thank the person who will be forever immortalised as Poor Chris. Since my 2019 road trip, he has been dragged down into a coal mine on the outskirts of Liège and forced to visit many obscure villages throughout Europe in my quest to follow in Anne's footsteps. This is the same Poor Chris I tormented every day, and still continue to do so, by talking about Anne Lister much too often. And it is he whom I bribed with beer to check all my calculations for this book over and over again. Thank you, Poor Chris, for eating leftovers three times a week while I wrote this book.

I hope that this book will inspire readers to go out and explore the Continent just as Anne Lister did, and that her words contained in this book will make the experience extra special, as they have done for mine.

Appendix

Anne Lister's Itinerary

The following lists all the villages, cities and known places Anne visited, or saw from a distance, and described in her diary during her travels between 18 July (when she landed in Calais) and 12 December 1833 (when she left Cuxhaven), which the modern tourist may visit today. The cities are categorised within modern borders.

France (18 July – 22 August 1833)
Calais
Ardres
La Recousse
Saint-Omer
    Cathédrale Notre-Dame de Saint-Omer, Église Catholique Saint Denis à Saint-Omer, Palais de Justice de Saint-Omer

Aire-sur-la-Lys
Lillers
Pernes
St-Pol-sur-Ternoise
Frévent
Amiens
> *Cathédrale Notre-Dame d'Amiens, Palais de Justice d'Amiens*

Hébécourt
Flers-sur-Noye
Breteuil
St Just en Chaussée
Wavignies
Clermont (Oise)
> *Donjon de Clermont*

Laigneville
Chantilly
> *Château de Chantilly, Domaine de Chantilly, Musée du Cheval (former royal stables), Église Notre-Dame de l'Assomption de Chantilly, Jardins du Château de Chantilly, Île d'amour, Château de la Reine Blanche (Coye la Forêt)*

Luzarches
Écouen
> *Musée National de la Renaissance (former Château Écouen)*

Paris
> *Rue Cambon (formerly Rue Neuve de Luxembourg until 1879). Anne stayed at No. 4 Rue Neuve de Luxembourg, on the third floor while in Paris), Jardin des Tuileries, Champs*

Élysées, l'île de la Cité, Temple Protestant de l'Oratoire du Louvre, Hôtel Le Meurice, 228 Rue de Rivoli (Anne visited Lady Gordon who was staying at Meurice's), Eglise Saint Roch
Meaux
Cathédrale Saint-Étienne de Meaux
St-Jean-les-Deux Jumeaux
La Ferté-sous-Jouarre
Château Thierry
Épernay
Moët et Chandon
Châlons
Cathédrale St-Etienne de Châlons-en-Champagne, Hôtel de Ville de Châlons, Collégiale Notre-Dame en Vaux, Basilique Notre-Dame de L'Epine
Somme-Vesle
Orbéval
Sainte-Menehould
Clermont-en-Argonne
Verdun
Cathédrale Notre-Dame de Verdun, Centre Mondial de la Paix (former episcopal palace), Citadelle Haute, Porte Saint Paul, Dragées Braquier
Étain
Spincourt
Longuyon
Longwy

In the Footsteps of Anne Lister

Luxembourg (22 – 23 August 1833)
Bascharage
Luxembourg
   Place d'Armes, Cathédrale Notre-Dame, Casemates du Bock
Grevenmacher

Germany (23 August – 17 September 1833)
Igel
   Igeler Säule (Roman sandstone column, burial monument of the Secundinier cloth merchant family)
Trier
   Porta Nigra, Römerbrücke, Rotes Haus, Hauptmarkt, Liebfrauenkirche, Dom Trier, St Paulinus, Kaiserthermen, Museum am Dom Trier (former prison), Trier Amphitheatre, Kurfürstliches Palais, ehemalige Abteikirche St Maximin (former abbey, was barracks when Anne was in Trier)
Hetzerath
Wittlich
Lützerath
Kaisersesch
   Church on Baldiunstraße
Polch
Koblenz
   Festung Ehrenbreitstein (visited in 1829), Basilika Sankt Kastor, Kastorbrunnen also known as Napoleonsbrunnen on Kastorhof

Montabaur
   Schloss Montabaur
Limburg
   Dom zu Limburg, Alte Lahnbrücke Limburg
Weilburg
   Schloss Weilburg
Braunfels
   Schloss Braunfels
Wetzlar
   Wetzlarer Dom, Ruine Kalsmunt, Säuturm Wetzlar
Klein Linden
Gießen
Staufenberg
   Burgruine Staufenberg
Sicherthausen
Bellnhausen
Marburg
   Landgrafenschloss, Elisabethkirche
Schönstadt
Halsdorf
Jesberg
   Burg Jesberg
Kerstenhausen
Wabern
Dissen

Kassel
Fridericianum, Wilhelmshöhe, Herkules, Löwenburg, Marmorbad, Planetarium und Astronomisch-Physikalisches Kabinett (former orangerie)

Hannoversch Münden

Dransfeld

Göttingen
Georg August Universität Göttingen

Northeim

Salzderhelden

Einbeck
Altes Rathaus, Marktkirche St Jacobi Einbeck

Ammensen

Brüggen

Thiedenwiese

Hanover
Waterloosäule (Waterloo column), Herrenhausen Gärten, Schloss Herrenhausen, Marktkirche Hannover, Leibnizhaus, Altes Rathaus, Leibniztempel

Neustadt am Rübenberge
Liebfrauenkirche

Nienburg

Asendorf

Memsen

Syke

Bremen
Dom Bremen, Bleikeller, Altes Rathaus, Ratskeller (Rosenkeller, Apostelkeller), Domplatz
Ottersberg
Rotenburg
Tostedt
Harburg
Hamburg
Altona, Jungfernstieg, Christianskirche – Klopstock's tomb, Rainvilleterrasse, Börsentag Hamburg, Stintfang, St Michaelis Kirche, St Petri Kirche, Nikolaikirche, Altes Rathaus
Wandsbek
Ahrensburg
Schloss Ahrensburg
Bad Oldesloe
Peter-Paul Kirche
Lübeck
Puppenbrücke, Holstentor, Markt, Marienkirche, Altes Rathaus, Domkirche, St Petri Kirche, Prahl Denkmal, Heiligen Geist Hospital, Burgtor, Israeldorf (day trip), Breite Straße (specifically mentioned in diary, where she walked and shopped)

St Anne's Museum (to see the old statues from Puppenbrücke and the remains of the ancient astronomical clock)
Israeldorf
Travemünde
Alter Leuchtturm Travemünde

Denmark (18 September – 3 December 1833)
Copenhagen
Vor Frue Kirke, Rundetårn, Christiansborg Slot, Ved Stranden 18 (former Hotel Royal), Amalienborg, Amaliegade, Langelinie, Rosenborg Slot, Frederiksberg Have, Børsen, island of Amager, Elsinore Gate Østerport, Frederiksdal House, Kastellet, Nyhaven

Thorvaldsen's Museum (for Bertel Thorvaldsen's work)
Outskirts of Copenhagen
Eremitageslottet, Charlottenlund, Glostrup
Roskilde
Domkirke
Ryegård
Ryegaard og Trudsholm Godser
Lejre
Ledreborg Castle
Ringsted
Korsør
Korsør Town & Crossing Museum (for the model of Mercurius which Anne used to cross the Storebælt), Old Port
Nyborg
Odense
Middelfart
Middelfart Kirke, Gammelhavn (old port)
Snoghøj
Kolding
Koldinghus

Haderslev
Haderslev Domsogn
Åbenrå

Germany (3 – 12 December 1833)
Flensburg
Schleswig
Schloss Gottorf
Rendsburg
Bad Bramstedt
Hamburg
Altona, Nobistor, Nikolaifleet (old port between 1188 and 1863)
Cuxhaven
Hamburger Leuchtturm Cuxhaven, Alte Liebe pier, Schloss Ritzebüttel

About the Author

Adeline Lim travels in Anne Lister's footsteps. She has travelled to more than sixty countries, but has difficulty recalling how travel had inspired her before she learnt of Anne Lister. She also spends too much of her time transcribing Anne's travel journals and diaries. She currently lives in Bonn, Germany with her neglected and long-suffering husband, Chris. She has tormented him with her various obsessions, following in the footsteps of Alexander the Great and other celebrated personalities for nearly twenty years.

In the past year, when her obsession with Anne Lister's adventures commenced, poor Chris has been further tormented by Adeline's non-stop travel narration.

Unfortunately for him, Adeline's information and travel narration are nearly two hundred years out of date.

Nowadays, Adeline drags Chris to the most obscure villages, down into the deepest and darkest mines and up tremendous mountains. Dinner conversation generally revolves around where Adeline (and poor Chris) might travel to next.

Anne Lister travel enthusiasts can discover the world with Adeline on Twitter (@laFemmeAd). Photos relating to the 1833 journey are available on Flickr (https://www.flickr.com/photos/anne_lister_travels/)

Printed in Great Britain
by Amazon